THE NEW
Cook Light
& eat right COOKBOOK

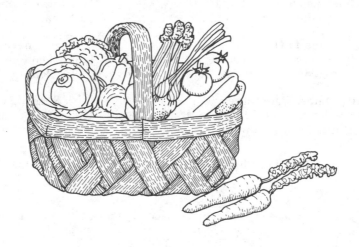

FAVORITE RECIPES® PRESS

CREDITS

Great American Opportunities, Inc./Favorite Recipes® Press

President: Thomas F. McDow III

Editorial Manager: Mary Jane Blount
Editors: Georgia Brazil, Mary Cummings, Jane Hinshaw, Linda Jones,
Marian Sherman, Mary Wilson
Typography: Pam Newsome, Sara Anglin

Home Economics Advisory Board

Favorite Recipes® Press wants to recognize the following persons who
graciously serve on our Home Economics Advisory Board:

Cover Photograph: The Sugar Association, Inc.

Published by: Favorite Recipes® Press, a division of
Great American Opportunities, Inc.
P. O. Box 305142
Nashville, TN 37230

Manufactured in the United States of America
First Printing: 1990, 41,000 copies
Second Printing: 1991, 33,000 copies

Copyright© 1990 by Great American Opportunities
Library of Congress Catalog Number: 89-71433
ISBN: 0-87197-269-7

Recipes for photograph on cover are on pages 63 and 94.

IT'S HAPPENING IN HOME ECONOMICS!!

Thomas F. McDow III
President

The traditional skills we associate with home economics education have been updated to serve American life today. For instance, "cooking" today includes quick, quality menu selection and easy meal preparation, time-saving recipes, cooking with convenience foods, adapting good nutrition to changing life-styles, and involving other family members in food planning, selection and preparation.

And, in addition, home economics is addressing some of the most significant challenges facing America today—extended and single-parent families, home and family management, resource management and conservation, alcohol and drug abuse, consumer education, nutrition and health, teen pregnancy, AIDS and other sexually transmitted diseases.

We at Favorite Recipes® Press are proud to have worked hand-in-hand with home economics teachers publishing Home Economics Teachers Cookbooks for over 25 years. The sale of these books in community service projects has raised more than $50,000,000 in profits for home economics departments all across America.

We hope you continue to enjoy Home Economics Teachers Cookbooks, both the time-tested cookbooks on your shelf, and the new books in the series. The new cookbooks contain nutritional analysis, quick, easy and healthy dishes, many recipes that use basic ingredients already on hand, balanced meals and menus that are fun and easy to prepare by any member of the household, and many more features to fit modern American life-styles.

We hope, too, that you continue to support your local home economics teachers and students in their programs and activities. It is, indeed, happening in today's home economics!

Tom McDow

Thomas F. McDow III
President

INTRODUCTION

The author of a recent cookbook wisely noted that, until recent years, cookbooks told us how to cook, but not what to cook, or why. If you've looked recently at one of your old tried-and-true recipe collections, you'll probably second that notion. While many of us grew up learning how to make—and eat—mouth-watering cakes, casseroles and breads, we paid little attention to what went in them or whether they were good for our health.

A cup of lard? Virtually a necessity in some baked goods. White sugar? A must if you were planning stewed tomatoes or spaghetti sauce. A big, well-marbled cut of beef? The best that money could buy. And salt? The more the merrier—after all, how else could you bring out the true flavor of food?

The idea behind old-fashioned home cooking was that if it tasted good, it was good. After all, if Mom made it, it had to be good for you, right? For most people, a good home-cooked meal meant a large portion of meat, usually red, or chicken, frequently fried, potatoes cooked with butter or cheese in some combination, vegetables boiled to a comforting mush with lots of salt or heavy sauces, buttery bread and rolls, a nice big glass of creamy milk topped off with a generous slice of cake or pie and maybe a little ice cream.

Now admittedly that kind of menu still has its charms, and for many of us may even be the ultimate dream meal. But the point, of course, is that the past two decades have pointed out some pretty large holes in the good/good-for-you line of reasoning we held so dear for so long. A good many of those very things Mom tempted our palates with turned out to be not so good for us in later years, as medical research looked closely at how lifestyle influences heart disease, high blood pressure and even cancer.

As a group, Americans have embraced a whole new approach to food in recent years. Nutrition is no longer just a word used by the school nurse or dietitian in her annual basic-food-groups lecture. Today, eating well means eating healthy.

We're much more conscious than ever before of the importance of eating light and eating right, whether we're watching our weight, paying attention to our health, or simply enjoying the feeling of well-being we get when we're eating properly. But we're not quite ready to trade our turkey and dressing for tofu, or our stuffed baked potato for plain brown rice.

As cooks, we want to feed our families the best meals we can, food that we feel confident is nutritious, but at the same time delicious and appealing to the whole family.

We want readily available ingredients, not just the kind we find only at the health-food store or through a fancy mail-order catalog. We want recipes that are easy to understand and uncomplicated in technique, and that don't keep us in the kitchen all day.

These days, fortunately, eating light is a pleasure. Take a look at that old cookbook again, and pay close attention to the amounts of salt, refined sugar, saturated fats and high-cholesterol meats and cheeses you'll find there.

Now take a look at a new cookbook, not the diet variety, but an ordinary cookbook. You'll find less salt, far less lard, butter and animal fat, much smaller amounts of sugar and a new emphasis on lean meats, fish and other seafood, a wide variety of fresh vegetables and fruits and lower-fat and lower-sodium cheeses. Chances are, you'd never miss some of those old heavyweight ingredients, and you may have already dropped them from your own family recipes in favor of their lighter equivalents.

Today we are able to enjoy a tremendous variety and availability of ingredients in our local supermarkets. Nearly everybody, no matter what part of the country they live in, can fill their baskets full of fresh fish, bounteous fresh produce even in the winter, exotic fruits, fresh herbs and spices, a myriad of low-fat dairy products, whole grain flour and other delights that were unheard of twenty years ago.

Add to that the ever-increasing number of stores that boast fresh salad bars, fresh homemade pasta, freshly squeezed juices, exotic fresh shellfish, homemade bread, even vegetarian pizza bars next to the video counter, and it's clear that healthy eating never had it so good!

In *Cook Light & Eat Right*, you'll find dozens of outstanding recipes that pass both the "good" and "good for you" tests—both of equal importance for the way we eat today. They'll help you take advantage of the great selection of food that's out there, give you a few pointers on nutrition and at the same time give you results you'll be proud to serve your family and guests.

We don't pretend that these recipes will help you shed pounds or regain your girlish figure, but they do present tasty, healthier alternatives to liven up your day-to-day menus, even if the mere mention of "bean sprout" foments rebellion among your troops.

We hope you'll find this book a great starting place if you're just beginning to cook light and eat right, and a healthy and delicious addition to your repertoire if you've already seen the "light."

NUTRITIONAL ANALYSIS GUIDELINES

The editors have attempted to present these family recipes in a form that allows approximate nutritional values to be computed. Persons with dietary or health problems or whose diets require close monitoring should not rely solely on the nutritional information provided. They should consult their physician or a registered dietitian for specific information.

Abbreviations for Nutritional Analysis

Cal — Calories	T Fat — Total Fat	Sod — Sodium
Prot — Protein	Chol — Cholesterol	gr — gram
Carbo — Carbohydrates	Potas — Potassium	mg — milligram

Nutritional information for recipes is computed from values furnished by the United States Department of Agriculture Handbook. Many specialty items and new products now available on the market are not included in this handbook. However, producers of new products frequently publish nutritional information on each product's packaging and that information may be added, as applicable, for a more complete analysis. If the nutritional analysis notes the exclusion of a particular ingredient, check the package information for nutritional content.

Unless otherwise specified, the nutritional analysis of these recipes is based on all measurements being level.

- Artificial sweeteners vary in use and strength so should be used "to taste," using the recipe ingredients as a guideline.
- Artificial sweeteners using aspartame (NutraSweet and Equal) should not be used as a sweetener in recipes involving prolonged heating which reduces the sweet taste. For further information on the use of these sweeteners, refer to package information.
- Alcoholic ingredients have been analyzed for the basic ingredients, although cooking causes the evaporation of alcohol thus decreasing caloric content.
- Buttermilk, sour cream, and yogurt are commercial types.
- Cake mixes prepared using package directions include 3 eggs and 1/2 cup oil.
- Chicken, cooked for boning and chopping, has been roasted; this method yields the lowest caloric values.
- Cottage cheese is cream-style with 4.2% creaming mixture. Dry-curd cottage cheese has no creaming mixture.
- Eggs are all large.
- Flour is unsifted all-purpose flour.
- Garnishes, serving suggestions and other optional additions and variations are not included in the analysis.
- Margarine and butter are regular, not whipped or presoftened.
- Milk is whole milk, 3.5% butterfat. Lowfat milk is 1% butterfat. Evaporated milk is whole milk with 60% of the water removed.
- Oil is any type of vegetable cooking oil, unless otherwise specified. Shortening is hydrogenated vegetable shortening.
- Salt and other ingredients to taste as noted in the method have not been included in the nutritional analysis.
- If a choice of ingredients has been given, the nutritional analysis reflects the first option only.

TABLE OF CONTENTS

APPETIZERS & SOUPS

If there's one type of food that would seem completely incompatible with light eating, it's probably those mouth-watering appetizers and hors d'oeuvres we all love to nibble on.

Now it's pretty hard to convincingly argue that appetizers are necessary to sustain existence. But they're still one of life's pleasures, and there's no reason to give them up, since now we can create healthy versions of those calorie and cholesterol-laden goodies we've come to know on party tables.

You'll discover a basket of new ways to treat familiar themes in the section that follows. For example, in dip recipes that call for sour cream (500 calories per 8 ounces), consider using low-fat cottage cheese (180 calories) or plain yogurt (130 calories). You can even substitute low-fat cottage cheese for half the avocado (high in cholesterol and fat) in guacamole.

As for dippers, avoid those high-fat, high-salt chips and crackers. For healthier snacking, slice pita bread rounds horizontally, then stack and cut into wedges, or do the same with tortillas. Simply spread on a cookie sheet, toast in a hot oven for a few minutes, and serve.

You've probably worn out the old carrot and celery sticks, so why not switch to colorful "new" vegetables for appetizers, such as zucchini or cucumber "fingers," red and green pepper strips, cherry tomatoes, whole button mushrooms or blanched pea pods or broccoli flowerets?

Soups have always been a favorite with health-conscious cooks. To update your old favorites, try low-sodium, low-fat canned broths for a soup base instead of high-fat stocks. Cut down on salt, substituting fresh herbs and spices or seasoned "no salt" blends.

Slow-cooking soups and stews are a great place to use lean cuts of beef. Soups featuring legumes such as lentils and peas are a great source of both low-fat protein and fiber, but be sure to use fresh beans. The canned variety can have 40 times more sodium than the dried variety. Before serving, always skim the fat from soups. And for an extra-healthy touch, sprinkle a little extra bran fiber in soups and stews.

Whether you're looking for innovative ways to kick off a party menu or satisfying soups to warm a cold winter day, you'll find healthy and delicious ideas in the pages that follow.

Appetizers & Soups

ANTIPASTO

1 cup oil
1/2 cup red wine vinegar
1 tablespoon garlic powder
3 tablespoons honey
1 tablespoon pickle relish
1   4-ounce jar chopped
    pimentos, drained
1   8-ounce can whole green
    beans, drained
1   2 1/4-ounce can sliced black
    olives, drained
1   8-ounce can garbanzo beans,
    drained
1   5-ounce jar stuffed green
    olives, drained
1 green bell pepper, cut into
    1/2-inch pieces
Flowerets of 1 small head
    cauliflower

Yield: 115 tablespoons

Combine oil, vinegar, garlic powder, honey, pickle relish and salt and pepper to taste in bowl; mix well. Combine pimentos, green beans, black olives, garbanzo beans, green olives, green pepper and cauliflower in large bowl; toss to mix. Add oil mixture; toss to coat. Marinate, covered, in refrigerator for 4 to 5 days, tossing twice daily. Drain before serving.

Approx Per Tablespoon: Cal 26; Prot 0.3 g;
Carbo 1.5 g; T Fat 2.3 g; Chol 0.0 mg;
Potas 19.0 mg; Sod 40.1 mg.

Gillian West, Pennsylvania

MINIATURE BEEF TURNOVERS

8 ounces ground beef
1 envelope beef-flavored
    mushroom gravy mix
1 cup drained bean sprouts
1/2 cup sliced water chestnuts
2 tablespoons chopped onion
2   8-count packages
refrigerator crescent rolls

Yield: 32 turnovers

Brown ground beef with gravy mix, bean sprouts, water chestnuts and onion in skillet, stirring until ground beef is crumbly; drain. Separate crescent rolls into triangles. Cut triangles into halves. Place 1 spoonful of ground beef mixture in center of each triangle. Fold over filling; press edges to seal. Place on ungreased baking sheet. Bake at 375 degrees for 15 minutes or until golden brown.

Approx Per Turnover: Cal 76; Prot 2.4 g;
Carbo 7.6 g; T Fat 4.0 g; Chol 4.9 mg;
Potas 51.4 mg; Sod 295.0 mg.

Linda Curry, Delaware

Surprise Cheese Puffs

1 cup shredded Cheddar cheese
1/4 cup margarine, softened
1/2 cup flour
1/2 teaspoon paprika
24 small pimento-stuffed olives

Yield: 24 servings

Combine cheese and margarine in bowl; mix with fork until well blended. Add flour and paprika; mix well. Pat olives dry with paper towels. Shape 1 teaspoon cheese mixture around each olive, covering completely; arrange on baking sheet. Freeze until firm. Store in freezer containers or plastic bags. Place frozen olive balls on baking sheet. Bake at 425 degrees for 15 to 20 minutes or until light brown. Reduce baking time to 8 to 10 minutes if olive balls are not frozen before baking.

Approx Per Serving: Cal 50; Prot 1.5 g; Carbo 2.1 g; T Fat 4.1 g; Chol 5.0 mg; Potas 11.2 mg; Sod 148.0 mg.

Martha Markham, West Virginia

Aunt El's Nut and Cheese Ring

5 cups shredded sharp Cheddar cheese
3/4 cup margarine, softened
2 tablespoons Dijon mustard
2 teaspoons Worcestershire sauce
1 teaspoon Sherry
1/2 cup chopped dried apricots
1/2 cup whole pecans

Yield: 50 servings

Combine first 5 ingredients in bowl; mix well. Grease 7-inch ring mold with oil. Sprinkle apricots and pecans in bottom of prepared ring mold. Press cheese mixture into mold. Cover with plastic wrap. Chill overnight. Unmold onto serving plate. Serve with crackers.

Approx Per Serving: Cal 82; Prot 3.0 g; Carbo 1.3 g; T Fat 7.3 g; Chol 11.9 mg; Potas 37.6 mg; Sod 112.0 mg.

Bonnie Eastwood, New Jersey

Zippy Cheese Roll

8 ounces light cream cheese, softened
1/4 cup Parmesan cheese
1 teaspoon horseradish
1/3 cup chopped green olives
1   2 1/2-ounce package chipped dried beef, finely chopped

Yield: 32 tablespoons

Combine cream cheese, Parmesan cheese, horseradish, olives and dried beef in bowl; mix well. Shape into roll. Chill for 1 hour. Serve with assorted crackers.

Approx Per Tablespoon: Cal 28; Prot 1.6 g; Carbo 0.3 g; T Fat 2.3 g; Chol 9.6 mg; Potas 20.5 mg; Sod 175.0 mg.

Jacqueline Marlin, Virginia

Microwave Stuffed Clams

1/3 cup finely minced onion
2²/3 tablespoons butter
1   8-ounce can clams
Fine crumbs of 5 or 6 slices
bread
Finely chopped parsley to taste
Finely chopped green bell
pepper to taste

Yield: 10 servings

Microwave onion and butter in large covered bowl on High for 1¹/2 to 2 minutes or until transparent. Drain clams reserving juice. Mince clams. Add clams, crumbs and enough clam juice to moisten onion mixture. Mix in parsley and green pepper. Spoon into clam shells or custard cups. Arrange in circle in microwave. Microwave on High for 2 minutes. Rearrange clam shells. Microwave for 2 minutes longer.

Approx Per Serving: Cal 95; Prot 6.9 g;
Carbo 7.6 g; T Fat 4.0 g; Chol 23.4 mg;
Potas 165.0 mg; Sod 113.0 mg.

Barbara Palladino, Alabama

Broiled Crab Bites

1   7-ounce can crab meat
1/2 cup margarine, softened
1   5-ounce jar Old English
cheese
2 tablespoons mayonnaise
1/2 teaspoon seasoned salt
6 English muffins, split

Yield: 72 servings

Combine first 5 ingredients in bowl; mix well. Spread on muffin halves. Cut each muffin half into 6 triangles. Freeze in airtight container until firm. Place on 10x15-inch baking sheet. Broil for 5 to 10 minutes or until puffy and golden brown.

Approx Per Serving: Cal 35; Prot 1.4 g;
Carbo 2.4 g; T Fat 2.2 g; Chol 3.9 mg;
Potas 44.2 mg; Sod 95.9 mg.

Maria Winston, Louisiana

Herbed Yogurt Cheese Dip

16 ounces plain nonfat yogurt
1/4 cup reduced-calorie
mayonnaise
1 tablespoon dillweed, crushed
3/4 teaspoon garlic powder
3/4 teaspoon onion powder
1/8 teaspoon salt
1/8 teaspoon pepper

Yield: 36 tablespoons

Line large strainer with double thickness of 18x20-inch cheesecloth; place strainer over large bowl. Combine all ingredients in bowl; mix well. Spoon mixture into prepared strainer. Pull up corners of cheesecloth, twisting to enclose yogurt completely. Place in strainer in refrigerator. Let stand in refrigerator for 24 hours or until all liquid has drained into bowl and yogurt is of spreadable consistency. Place cheese on serving plate, discarding cheesecloth and liquid. Serve with bite-sized vegetables and crackers.

Approx Per Tablespoon: Cal 12; Prot 1.0 g;
Carbo 1.0 g; T Fat 1.0 g; Chol 1.0 mg;
Potas 0 mg; Sod 7.0 mg.

Joan Schneider, Oregon

GUACAMOLE DIP

1 small tomato
1 cup mashed avocado
1/4 cup mayonnaise
1 tablespoon lemon juice
1/4 cup finely chopped onion
2 tablespoons finely chopped
green chilies

Yield: 8 servings

Chop tomato finely; drain well. Blend avocado, mayonnaise and lemon juice in bowl. Stir in tomato, onion and green chilies. Chill, covered, for 1 hour. Serve with sliced fresh vegetables and corn chips for dipping.

Approx Per Serving: Cal 102; Prot 0.9 g;
Carbo 3.7 g; T Fat 9.9 g; Chol 4.1 mg;
Potas 225.0 mg; Sod 44.0 mg.

Francie Jenkins, Ohio

NOBODY KNOWS RELISH DIP

2 4-ounce cans chopped
green chilies
4 ounces green salad
olives, chopped
3 or 4 green onions, chopped
3 or 4 tomatoes, chopped
2 tablespoons wine vinegar
1 tablespoon oil
2 jalapeño peppers, chopped

Yield: 12 servings

Combine green chilies, olives, green onions, tomatoes, vinegar, oil and jalapeño peppers in bowl; mix well. Add salt and pepper to taste. Serve with tortilla chips.

Approx Per Serving: Cal 33; Prot 0.7 g;
Carbo 2.9 g; T Fat 2.7 g; Chol 0.0 mg;
Potas 110.0 mg; Sod 240.0 mg.

Diane Lyons, Missouri

LIGHT AND EASY SPINACH DIP

1 10-ounce package frozen
spinach, thawed
1/4 cup dry vegetable soup mix
1 1/3 cups nonfat yogurt
1/3 cup light sour cream
1/4 cup light mayonnaise
1 8-ounce can water chestnuts,
drained, chopped
2 tablespoons chopped green
onions

Yield: 64 tablespoons

Combine spinach, soup mix, yogurt, sour cream, mayonnaise, water chestnuts and green onions in large bowl; mix well. Chill for 1 hour. Serve with assorted crackers.

Approx Per Tablespoon: Cal 11; Prot 0.5 g;
Carbo 1.5 g; T Fat 0.4 g; Chol 1.0 mg;
Potas 33.2 mg; Sod 42.4 mg.

Sandi Edelston, New Mexico

Mushroom Hors D'oeuvres

1 pound mushrooms, chopped
1 onion, finely chopped
1/4 cup margarine, softened
12 ounces cream cheese, softened
1 1/2 teaspoons Worcestershire sauce
1/4 teaspoon garlic salt
1   16-ounce loaf Pepperidge Farm thinly sliced white bread
1/4 cup margarine, softened
1/4 cup Parmesan cheese

Yield: 40 small sandwiches

Sauté mushrooms and onion in margarine in skillet until onions are transparent. Add cream cheese, Worcestershire sauce and garlic salt; mix well. Spread over 10 bread slices. Butter 1 side of 10 bread slices. Place margarine side up on mushroom mixture. Sprinkle with Parmesan cheese. Cut each sandwich into quarters. Arrange on 10x15-inch baking sheet. Bake at 350 degrees for 10 minutes or until mixture is bubbly.

Approx Per Sandwich: Cal 87; Prot 2.1 g; Carbo 6.6 g; T Fat 5.9 g; Chol 9.7 mg; Potas 73.8 mg; Sod 127.0 mg.

Judy Kennaugh, Arizona

Cold Spiced Shrimp

3/4 cup chicken broth
2 tablespoons cider vinegar
2 tablespoons white wine
1 teaspoon sugar
3 tablespoons catsup
2 tablespoons oil
2 green onions, chopped
1/4 teaspoon ginger
1/8 teaspoon cayenne pepper
1 pound cooked shrimp, peeled

Yield: 12 servings

Combine chicken broth, vinegar, wine, sugar, catsup, oil, green onions, ginger and cayenne pepper in large bowl; mix well. Add shrimp. Chill for 1 hour. Serve with toothpicks or arrange on lettuce leaves.

Approx Per Serving: Cal 70; Prot 8.4 g; Carbo 2.1 g; T Fat 2.8 g; Chol 74.0 mg; Potas 122.7 mg; Sod 178.0 mg.

Beverly Mangun, Indiana

Spinach Hors D'oeuvres

1/2 cup melted margarine
1 cup milk
2 eggs, beaten
1 cup whole wheat flour
1 teaspoon baking powder
1   10-ounce package frozen chopped spinach, thawed
1/2 cup chopped onion
1/2 cup shredded Cheddar cheese

Yield: 36 appetizers

Blend first 3 ingredients in large bowl. Add flour and baking powder; mix well. Fold in well-drained spinach, onion and cheese. Spoon into 9x13-inch baking pan sprayed with nonstick cooking spray. Bake at 375 degrees for 30 minutes or until brown. Cut into 1 1/2x2-inch pieces. Serve warm.

Approx Per Appetizer: Cal 52; Prot 1.7 g; Carbo 3.4 g; T Fat 3.7 g; Chol 17.8 mg; Potas 55.0 mg; Sod 62.0 mg.

Peggy Armstrong, Utah

CHEESY SPINACH PUFFS

1 10-ounce package frozen chopped spinach, thawed
1/2 cup chopped onion
2 eggs, slightly beaten
1/2 cup Parmesan cheese
1/2 cup shredded Cheddar cheese
1/2 cup blue cheese salad dressing
1/4 cup margarine, melted
1/2 teaspoon garlic powder
1 8-ounce package corn muffin mix

Yield: 60 puffs

Combine spinach and onion in glass bowl. Microwave on High until tender. Drain well; squeeze dry. Combine eggs, cheeses, salad dressing, margarine and garlic powder in bowl; mix well. Add spinach mixture and corn muffin mix; mix well. Chill, covered, for several hours. Shape into 1-inch balls. Chill or freeze, wrapped, until serving time. Place on 10x15-inch baking sheet. Bake chilled puffs at 350 degrees for 10 to 12 minutes or frozen puffs for 12 to 15 minutes.

Approx Per Puff: Cal 33; Prot 1.0 g; Carbo 1.9 g; T Fat 2.4 g; Chol 11.4 mg; Potas 24.9 mg; Sod 59.3 mg.

Ruth Parkinson, Colorado

AVOCADO AND SALMON SPREAD

1 large avocado, mashed
1 8-ounce can salmon, drained, mashed
1/2 cup ricotta cheese
1/4 cup thinly sliced green onion
1 green bell pepper, seeded, finely chopped
Garlic powder to taste
2 teaspoons prepared mustard
1 teaspoon prepared horseradish
1/8 teaspoon lemon pepper

Yield: 48 tablespoons

Combine avocado, salmon, ricotta cheese, green onion, green pepper, garlic powder, mustard, horseradish and lemon pepper in bowl; mix well. Spoon into serving bowl. Garnish with light sprinkling of alfalfa sprouts. Serve with assorted crackers and alfalfa sprouts on the side.

Approx Per Tablespoon: Cal 19; Prot 1.4 g; Carbo 0.6 g; T Fat 1.3 g; Chol 3.9 mg; Potas 57.0 mg; Sod 7.2 mg.

Marilynn Ashmore, North Dakota

CHEESE SPREAD

8 ounces light cream cheese, softened
1 8-ounce can crushed pineapple, drained
1 2 1/2-ounce package dried beef, chopped
1/3 cup chopped chives

Yield: 42 tablespoons

Combine all ingredients in bowl; mix well. Chill in refrigerator. Serve with crackers.

Approx Per Tablespoon: Cal 25; Prot 0.9 g; Carbo 0.9 g; T Fat 2.0 g; Chol 8.6 mg; Potas 20.4 mg; Sod 74.5 mg.

Roberta England, Minnesota

ZUCCHINI APPETIZER

1 cup buttermilk baking mix
1 teaspoon baking powder
1/2 cup oil
4 eggs, beaten
3 cups grated zucchini
1/2 cup finely chopped onion
1/2 cup Parmesan cheese
2 tablespoons chopped parsley
1/2 teaspoon oregano
1 clove of garlic, minced

Yield: 64 squares

Combine baking mix and baking powder in bowl; mix well. Stir in oil and eggs. Add zucchini, onion, cheese, parsley, oregano, garlic and pepper to taste; mix well. Spread in 9x13-inch baking pan. Bake at 350 degrees for 30 minutes or until golden brown. Cut into small squares. Serve warm.

Approx Per Square: Cal 33; Prot 0.9 g;
Carbo 1.7 g; T Fat 2.5 g; Chol 17.6 mg;
Potas 25.5 mg; Sod 46.2 mg.

Christine Coleman, Michigan

FANTASTIC CHEESE POPCORN

3 tablespoons oil
1 teaspoon caraway, comino or mustard seed
1/3 cup unpopped popcorn
1 cup shredded Cheddar, Monterey Jack or Swiss cheese

Yield: 12 cups

Combine oil, desired seasoning seed and popcorn in popper. Pop according to manufacturer's instructions. Spread popped popcorn in buttered baking pan. Sprinkle with desired cheese. Bake at 350 degrees for 3 to 5 minutes. Season with salt to taste. Stir; serve immediately.

Approx Per Cup: Cal 98; Prot 3.3 g;
Carbo 6.1 g; T Fat 6.9 g; Chol 9.9 mg;
Potas 29.3 mg; Sod 58.9 mg.

Catherine Jones, Ohio

TEX-MEX MIX

2 teaspoons chili powder
2 teaspoons paprika
2 teaspoons cumin
2 quarts (popped in oil) popcorn
1 cup cubed Monterey Jack cheese

Yield: 8 servings

Mix chili powder, paprika and cumin in large bowl; mix well. Pour in hot popped popcorn; toss to mix. Add cheese cubes; mix well.

Approx Per Serving: Cal 131; Prot 5.5 g;
Carbo 6.1 g; T Fat 9.8 g; Chol 13.0 mg;
Potas 31.5 mg; Sod 76.4 mg.

Larrissa Charla, Washington

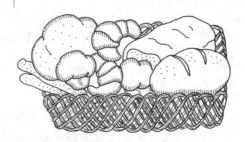

KIELBASA BEAN SOUP

1 medium potato, peeled,
chopped
2 carrots, sliced
1 medium onion, chopped
1/3 cup chopped celery
3 cups water
8 ounces kielbasa sausage,
thinly sliced
1 can bean with bacon soup

Yield: 12 servings

Combine potato, carrots, onion, celery and water in stockpot. Bring to a boil. Reduce heat. Simmer until tender. Add sausage and bean soup. Heat to serving temperature. This is a hearty "stick to your ribs" soup that smells delicious when you come in on a cold day.

Approx Per Serving: Cal 112; Prot 4.5 g; Carbo 9.3 g; T Fat 6.3 g; Chol 12.8 mg; Potas 233.0 mg; Sod 391.5 mg.

Carol Edwards, Kentucky

BEEF AND BARLEY SOUP

2 quarts water
1 meaty beef soupbone
1/2 cup chopped celery tops
1/2 teaspoon pepper
1/2 cup barley
3 cups coarsely chopped
cabbage
1 cup sliced carrots
1 cup sliced celery
2 cups thinly sliced onion
1 12-ounce can tomato paste

Yield: 10 servings

Combine water, soupbone, celery tops and pepper in stockpot. Bring to a boil. Reduce heat. Simmer, covered, for 1 to 2 hours. Remove bone. Cool slightly. Remove beef from bone. Return meat to stockpot. Add barley. Simmer for 30 minutes. Add cabbage, carrots, celery, onion and tomato paste. Simmer for 30 minutes or until vegetables are tender. This soup can be cooked in a Crock•Pot for 8 to 10 hours.

Approx Per Serving: Cal 140; Prot 6.2 g; Carbo 21.6 g; T Fat 4.2 g; Chol 11.6 mg; Potas 631.0 mg; Sod 62.0 mg.

Melanie McCoy, Vermont

BROCCOLI SOUP

1 tablespoon dried onion flakes
1/4 teaspoon white pepper
1 tablespoon flour
1 teaspoon basil
1 1/3 cups water
1 low-sodium chicken bouillon
cube
Flowerets of 1 pound broccoli
1 12-ounce can evaporated
milk

Yield: 4 cups

Combine onion flakes, white pepper, flour, basil, water, bouillon cube and salt to taste in saucepan. Stir in broccoli; cover. Bring to a boil; reduce heat. Simmer for 10 to 15 minutes or until broccoli is tender. Remove several flowerets and reserve for garnish. Spoon cooked mixture into blender container. Process until smooth. Return to saucepan. Stir in evaporated milk. Cook just until heated through. May substitute asparagus, mushrooms or zucchini for broccoli.

Approx Per Cup: Cal 102; Prot 6.9 g; Carbo 13.3 g; T Fat 3.5 g; Chol 0.0 mg; Potas 589.0 mg; Sod 372.0 mg.

Mary Bates, New Hampshire

CABBAGE SOUP

1 medium head cabbage,
chopped
6 large onions, chopped
1 large green bell pepper,
chopped
1 bunch celery, chopped
1   28-ounce can whole
tomatoes, chopped

Yield: 6 servings

Combine cabbage, onions, green pepper, celery, tomatoes and water to cover in soup pot; mix well. Bring to a boil. Cook for 10 minutes; reduce heat. Simmer for 2 1/2 to 3 hours or until flavors are well mixed. May add bouillon if desired.

Approx Per Serving: Cal 114; Prot 4.6 g; Carbo 25.1 g; T Fat 1.0 g; Chol 0.0 mg; Potas 1027.0 mg; Sod 333.0 mg.

Connie Kowalski, Illinois

EASY CHEESY CHOWDER

1 can cream of potato soup
1 can vegetarian vegetable soup
1 soup can each water and milk
1   15-ounce can cream-style
corn
1   15-ounce can mixed
vegetables
1 1/2 cups shredded Cheddar
cheese
1/2 teaspoon dillweed
1 teaspoon onion powder

Yield: 10 servings

Combine potato soup, vegetable soup, water and milk in saucepan; mix well. Add corn, mixed vegetables and cheese; mix well. Stir in dillweed and onion powder. Cook until heated through and cheese is melted.

Approx Per Serving: Cal 162; Prot 7.6 g; Carbo 17.2 g; T Fat 7.6 g; Chol 23.2 mg; Potas 291.0 mg; Sod 624.0 mg.

Jenny Parker, Idaho

CRAB SOUP

4 cups water
1 cup finely chopped carrots
1 cup chopped onion
3/4 cups chopped celery
1/4 cup margarine
1 tablespoon seafood seasoning
1 tablespoon Worcestershire
sauce
1 1/2 cups chopped potatoes
1   16-ounce can tomatoes
2 tablespoons chopped parsley
1 tablespoon flour
1/3 cup water
1   6-ounce can crab meat

Yield: 10 cups

Combine 4 cups water, carrots, onion, celery, margarine, seafood seasoning, Worcestershire sauce, potatoes, chopped tomatoes and parsley in soup pot. Simmer for 1 1/2 hours, stirring occasionally. Mix flour with 1/3 cup water. Stir into soup. Add crab meat. Simmer soup for 30 minutes, stirring occasionally.

Approx Per Cup: Cal 103; Prot 5.3 g; Carbo 9.4 g; T Fat 5.1 g; Chol 19.8 mg; Potas 330.0 mg; Sod 217.0 mg.

Melissa Haring, Nebraska

EGG DROP SOUP

2 13-ounce cans chicken broth
2 eggs, beaten
1/2 teaspoon sesame oil
3 green onions, chopped

Yield: 4 servings

Heat broth in saucepan almost to the boiling point. Add eggs gradually, stirring constantly. Remove from heat. Stir in oil. Sprinkle with green onions.

Approx Per Serving: Cal 51; Prot 3.5 g; Carbo 1.7 g; T Fat 3.4 g; Chol 137.0 mg; Potas 96.5 mg; Sod 35.5 mg.

Diane Monson, Maine

GAZPACHO

1 46-ounce can tomato juice
1/2 teaspoon pepper
2 tablespoons olive oil
2 tablespoons green taco sauce
1/4 cup wine vinegar
3 tomatoes, peeled, chopped
2 green bell peppers, chopped
2 cucumbers, peeled, chopped
5 green onions, chopped

Yield: 8 servings

Combine tomato juice, pepper, olive oil, taco sauce and vinegar in large container; mix well. Add tomatoes, green peppers, cucumbers and onions; mix well. Chill, covered, in refrigerator for 2 hours or until serving time. May serve hot if preferred.

Approx Per Serving: Cal 87; Prot 2.4 g; Carbo 13.5 g; T Fat 3.9 g; Chol 0.0 mg; Potas 645.0 mg; Sod 61.8 mg.

Barbara Windrow, Tennessee

LOUISIANA GUMBO

1/4 cup oil
1/2 cup flour
8 ounces smoked sausage
8 cups water
1 4-ounce jar oysters
1/2 pound chicken breast, chopped
8 ounces shrimp, peeled
4 ounces crab meat
1/2 teaspoon pepper
1/2 teaspoon Cajun seasoning
1 tablespoon chopped parsley
1 large onion, chopped
1 clove of garlic, minced

Yield: 10 servings

Heat oil in heavy skillet. Add flour; mix well. Cook until flour mixture browns, stirring constantly. Cut sausage into 1-inch pieces. Pour water into stockpot. Bring to a boil. Add flour mixture, sausage, oysters, chicken, shrimp and crab meat. Stir in pepper, Cajun seasoning, parsley, onion and garlic. Simmer for 2 1/2 hours or until chicken is tender.

Approx Per Serving: Cal 198; Prot 17.0 g; Carbo 6.0 g; T Fat 11.3 g; Chol 89.8 mg; Potas 207.0 mg; Sod 258.0 mg.

Ellen Thibodeaux, Louisiana

Instant Potato Soup

1 cup milk
2 cups water
2 tablespoons margarine
1/4 cup chopped onion
1/4 cup finely chopped celery
1/4 teaspoon pepper
2 cups instant potato flakes

Yield: 4 servings

Combine first 6 ingredients in 2-quart glass dish. Microwave on High for 3 minutes or until boiling. Stir in instant potato flakes. Let stand for 5 minutes. May serve cold if preferred.

Approx Per Serving: Cal 211; Prot 4.2 g; Carbo 19.6 g; T Fat 13.7 g; Chol 10.3 mg; Potas 365.0 mg; Sod 429.0 mg.

Anita Conover, Iowa

Healthy Veggie Soup

1 onion, chopped
3 carrots, thinly sliced
1 medium zucchini, chopped
2 cups chopped broccoli flowerets
2 cups chopped cauliflower
1 chicken bouillon cube
3 15-ounce cans chicken broth
1 16-ounce can stewed tomatoes
1 bay leaf

Yield: 6 servings

Combine first 7 ingredients in stockpot. Bring to a boil. Reduce heat. Simmer, covered, for 10 to 15 minutes. Add tomatoes, bay leaf, and salt and pepper to taste. Simmer until vegetables are tender. Remove bay leaf. Purée 1/2 cup vegetables in food processor container until smooth. Return puréed vegetables to stockpot. Cook for 15 minutes longer. May use low salt canned tomatoes and chicken broth to reduce sodium.

Approx Per Serving: Cal 106; Prot 8.9 g; Carbo 16.0 g; T Fat 1.8 g; Chol 0.9 mg; Potas 786.0 mg; Sod 1030.0 mg.

Sharon Kahn, South Dakota

Spring Vegetable Soup

2 carrots, sliced
1/2 cup cut green beans
1/2 cup peas
4 cups water
1 onion, chopped
2 tablespoons butter
2 stalks celery, chopped
1 teaspoon chopped parsley
1/2 red bell pepper, chopped
1/2 cup corn
1/2 teaspoon grated lemon rind

Yield: 5 servings

Combine carrots, beans, peas and water in saucepan. Bring to a boil. Simmer for 15 to 20 minutes or until vegetables are tender. Sauté onion in butter in skillet until tender. Add celery, parsley, bell pepper and corn to vegetable mixture. Simmer for 8 to 10 minutes. Stir in lemon rind, sautéed onion and salt and pepper to taste. Heat to serving temperature. Garnish with dillweed. This makes a great light supper when served with rye bread, fruit and cheeses. This soup should be made with only the most tender, young and fresh vegetables available.

Approx Per Serving: Cal 101; Prot 2.4 g; Carbo 13.2 g; T Fat 5.1 g; Chol 12.4 mg; Potas 308.0 mg; Sod 67.7 mg.

Rosanne Williams, Colorado

Salads

SALADS

A recent nutritional study came up with the astonishing fact that an average trip to your local restaurant salad bar, from which you return laden with lettuce, croutons, bacon bits, ham, cheese, marinated veggies and so on, will cost you around 1,000 calories. So much for the myth that salads are automatically good for you.

That doesn't mean, however, that to be healthful a salad must be restricted to wan bits of lettuce, cheerless vegetables, and lemon wedges. Salads can boast an almost infinite variety of ingredients, as the following recipes attest. And it's hard to beat the produce section for good nutrition.

Fruits and vegetables in general contain very little if any fat, no cholesterol, and no added sugar or salt. They're mostly carbohydrates and are a great source of fiber and vitamins. Cost-wise, they're a tremendous value for what they offer nutritionally, and taste-wise, what can compare to fresh farm produce?

When it comes to green salads (an excellent source of iron), keep in mind that dark green lettuces contain many more vitamins than iceberg lettuce. You might also consider "leafing" out into other greens, such as arugula, escarole, chicory and endive, or using fibrous vegetables such as broccoli, Brussels sprouts, cabbage and spinach into your salads. They're a rich source of Vitamin A and, according to the American Cancer Society, may play a role in reducing the likelihood of some kinds of cancer.

It is in the realm of salad dressings that many of us fall prey to unnecessarily bad habits. Pay attention to what type of oil you use in preparing salad dressings at home. Most vegetable oils contain about 100 calories per tablespoon, are polyunsaturated and have no cholesterol. Recently, though, a lot has been written about canola oil and that old standby, olive oil, which are monounsaturated and thought to be helpful in actually lowering blood cholesterol. If you don't like the taste of olive oil, watch for new "light" olive oils.

Many of us have now taken to oil-free salad dressings, using lemon or orange juice, herb vinegars and salt-free seasoning mixes and pepper. For creamy dressings, replace regular mayonnaise with low-calorie mayonnaise or remember low-fat cottage cheese (or buttermilk) and herbs whirled in a blender.

Our bountiful basket of salad and salad dressing ideas will help you serve fresh-from-the-garden creations that are light, easy and sure to become favorites at your house.

CRANBERRY WALDORF

1 3-ounce package lemon
gelatin
1 cup boiling cranberry juice
1 cup cranberry juice, chilled
1 cup chopped apples
1/2 cup chopped celery
1/4 cup chopped walnuts

Yield: 8 servings

Dissolve gelatin in boiling cranberry juice in bowl. Add chilled cranberry juice. Chill until partially set. Fold in apples, celery and walnuts. Pour into greased ring mold. Chill until firm. Unmold onto lettuce-lined serving plate. Serve with favorite salad dressing.

Approx Per Serving: Cal 109; Prot 1.6 g;
Carbo 21.4 g; T Fat 2.4 g; Chol 0.0 mg;
Potas 67.1 mg; Sod 43.0 mg.

Richie Stem, Nebraska

BEST-EVER FRUIT SALAD

1 16-ounce can pineapple
chunks, drained
4 Red Delicious apples,
chopped
4 cups green seedless grapes
1 pint strawberries
2 Navel oranges, peeled,
sectioned
16 ounces vanilla yogurt

Yield: 10 servings

Combine pineapple, apples, grapes, strawberries and oranges in salad bowl; mix well. Stir in yogurt gently. Serve in lettuce cups.

Approx Per Serving: Cal 131; Prot 1.4 g;
Carbo 32.9 g; T Fat 0.8 g; Chol 0.2 mg;
Potas 347.0 mg; Sod 5.7 mg.

Joy Walkman, Ohio

BUTTERMILK AND FRUIT SALAD MOLD

1 11-ounce can unsweetened
mandarin oranges
1 13-ounce can unsweetened
pineapple tidbits
1 6-ounce package sugar-free
orange gelatin
1 1/2 cups buttermilk
2 cups cottage cheese

Yield: 8 servings

Drain fruits, reserving juices. Add enough water to reserved juices to measure 1 1/2 cups. Bring juice mixture to a boil in saucepan; remove from heat. Add gelatin; stir until dissolved. Stir in buttermilk. Fold in cottage cheese. Pour into bowl; chill until partially set. Fold in fruit gently. Spoon into mold; chill until firm. Unmold onto serving plate.

Approx Per Serving: Cal 129; Prot 9.1 g;
Carbo 17.4 g; T Fat 2.7 g; Chol 9.4 mg;
Potas 203.0 mg; Sod 313.0 mg.

Lena Berry, Oklahoma

Golden Glow Salad

1 3-ounce package lemon
gelatin
1 cup boiling water
2¹/₂ cups crushed pineapple
Juice of 1 lemon
Juice of 1 orange
3 carrots, grated
Grated rind of 1 lemon
Grated rind of 1 orange

Yield: 8 servings

Dissolve gelatin in boiling water in bowl. Drain pineapple, reserving juice. Mix pineapple juice, lemon juice, orange juice and enough water to measure 1 cup. Stir into gelatin. Chill in refrigerator until partially set. Add pineapple, carrots, lemon and orange rind; mix well. Pour into oiled 6-cup mold. Chill until set. Unmold onto lettuce-lined serving plate.

Approx Per Serving: Cal 123; Prot 1.7 g; Carbo 31.0 g; T Fat 0.2 g; Chol 0.0 mg; Potas 206.0 mg; Sod 44.2 mg.

Wilma Reed, Iowa

Light Lime Salad

1 16-ounce can juice-pack
pineapple tidbits
1 small package sugar-free lime
gelatin
1 cup boiling water
1 cup low-fat cottage cheese
¹/₄ cup Sugar Twin artificial
sweetener

Yield: 9 servings

Drain pineapple, reserving juice. Dissolve gelatin in boiling water in small bowl. Add enough water to reserved juice to make 1 cup. Add to gelatin mixture; mix well. Chill until partially set. Stir in pineapple, cottage cheese and sweetener. Pour into 8-inch dish. Chill in refrigerator until firm.

Approx Per Serving: Cal 49; Prot 4.0 g; Carbo 7.2 g; T Fat 0.7 g; Chol 2.1 mg; Potas 81.0 mg; Sod 125.0 mg.

Carol Shane, Maryland

Melon Basket

1 small oval watermelon
2 cups cantaloupe balls
2 cups honeydew melon balls
2 cups fresh pineapple chunks
2 cups fresh raspberries or
strawberries
1 cup plain yogurt
2 tablespoons lemon juice
¹/₂ teaspoon poppy seed

Yield: 6 servings

Carve watermelon into basket, leaving handle. Scoop out 4 cups watermelon balls. Remove remaining watermelon pulp; drain basket shell. Combine watermelon balls with remaining fruit in bowl. Mix yogurt, lemon juice and poppy seed in small serving bowl. Chill watermelon basket, fruit and dressing until serving time. Spoon fruit into watermelon basket. Serve with yogurt-poppy seed dressing.

Approx Per Serving: Cal 79; Prot 4.3 g; Carbo 14.4 g; T Fat 1.0 g; Chol 2.5 mg; Potas 408.0 mg; Sod 242.0 mg.

Mary Rodgers, Alabama

PEACHES AND CREAM SALAD

1   3-ounce package lemon
       gelatin
1   3-ounce package orange
       gelatin
2 cups boiling water
2 cups vanilla ice cream,
       softened
4 peaches, peeled, sliced

Yield: 12 servings

Dissolve gelatins in boiling water in bowl. Spoon in ice cream, stirring until melted. Chill in refrigerator until partially set. Add peaches; mix well. Pour into serving dish. Chill until set.

Approx Per Serving: Cal 110; Prot 2.3 g; Carbo 21.0 g; T Fat 2.4 g; Chol 9.8 mg; Potas 99.8 mg; Sod 64.4 mg.

Emmaline Henry, California

PINEAPPLE AND COTTAGE CHEESE MOLD

2 teaspoons gelatin
3 tablespoons cold water
1 cup pineapple juice
2 tablespoons lemon juice
2 tablespoons sugar
1/2 cup crushed pineapple
1/3 cup finely chopped celery
1/3 cup cottage cheese

Yield: 8 servings

Soften gelatin in cold water in medium bowl. Heat mixture of pineapple and lemon juices just to the boiling point in saucepan. Add to gelatin; stir until dissolved. Stir in sugar. Chill until partially set. Fold in pineapple, celery and cottage cheese. Pour into mold. Chill until firm. Unmold onto serving plate.

Approx Per Serving: Cal 56; Prot 2.0 g; Carbo 11.4 g; T Fat 0.4 g; Chol 1.3 mg; Potas 84.9 mg; Sod 40.9 mg.

Delores Long, New York

PINEAPPLE SALAD

1   20-ounce can unsweetened
       crushed pineapple
1   3-ounce package sugar-free
       lemon gelatin
6 ounces light cream cheese,
       softened
1/3 cup chopped pecans
2 packages low-calorie topping
       mix
2 packets artificial sweetener
1 tablespoon lemon juice

Yield: 8 servings

Drain pineapple, reserving 1 cup juice. Heat reserved juice in saucepan. Add gelatin; stir until dissolved. Remove from heat. Beat cream cheese into gelatin mixture. Fold in pineapple. Chill until partially set. Fold in pecans, topping mix, sweetener and lemon juice. Pour into 8x8-inch dish. Chill until set.

Approx Per Serving: Cal 134; Prot 3.2 g; Carbo 12.8 g; T Fat 8.4 g; Chol 16.5 mg; Potas 133.0 mg; Sod 111.0 mg.

Bertha Edwards, Arkansas

CURRIED CHICKEN SALAD

4 cups chopped cooked chicken
1 8-ounce can sliced water
    chestnuts, drained
1 cup chopped celery
1 15-ounce can pineapple
    tidbits, drained
1 apple, cut into cubes
1 cup coarsely chopped walnuts
1 cup reduced-calorie
    mayonnaise
1 teaspoon soy sauce
1 tablespoon lemon juice
1/2 teaspoon pepper
1/2 teaspoon curry powder

Yield: 10 servings

Combine chicken, water chestnuts, celery, pineapple, apple and walnuts in bowl; mix well. Blend mayonnaise, soy sauce, lemon juice, pepper and curry powder in small bowl. Add to chicken mixture; mix lightly. Chill for 2 hours or longer. Serve on lettuce-lined plates. Garnish with additional pineapple. May add pinch of sugar to mayonnaise mixture if desired.

Approx Per Serving: Cal 292; Prot 19.6 g; Carbo 20.9 g; T Fat 14.9 g; Chol 53.6 mg; Potas 399.0 mg; Sod 212.0 mg.

Rosemary Moore, Oklahoma

CRAB SALAD IN ORANGE CUPS

4 large navel oranges
1/4 cup chopped fresh pineapple
8 ounces cooked crab meat
2 small green onions, chopped
1/2 cup finely chopped celery
1/4 cup mayonnaise
1 teaspoon fresh lemon juice
1/4 cup chopped almonds
4 lemon slices
4 parsley sprigs

Yield: 4 servings

Slice top off each orange. Scoop out and reserve orange pulp. Cut top edges of orange shells into zigzag pattern. Cut small slice from bottom of each so orange shells will stand upright. Set aside. Chop enough reserved orange pulp to measure 1/3 cup. Combine with pineapple, crab meat, green onions and celery in bowl. Add mayonnaise and lemon juice; mix well. Spoon into orange shells. Sprinkle with almonds. Garnish tops with twisted lemon slices and parsley sprigs.

Approx Per Serving: Cal 239; Prot 15.0 g; Carbo 24.1 g; T Fat 10.4 g; Chol 60.4 mg; Potas 575.0 mg; Sod 278.0 mg.

Jackie Glenn, Tennessee

RICE AND CRAB MEAT SALAD

2 cups cooked rice
1/2 pound cooked crab meat
1 8-ounce can sliced water
   chestnuts, drained
1/2 cup sliced celery
1/4 cup sliced green onions
1/4 cup yogurt
1/4 cup sour cream
1 tablespoon lemon juice
1/4 teaspoon hot pepper sauce

Yield: 4 servings

Combine rice, crab meat, water chestnuts, celery and onions in bowl; mix well. Combine yogurt, sour cream, lemon juice and hot pepper sauce in small bowl; mix well. Pour over rice mixture; toss lightly. Serve on lettuce-lined plate. Garnish with tomato wedges.

Approx Per Serving: Cal 243; Prot 15.5 g; Carbo 34.7 g; T Fat 4.4 g; Chol 63.9 mg; Potas 396.0 mg; Sod 198.0 mg.

Lucille Jones, Wisconsin

SEAFOOD PASTA SALAD

8 ounces tri-color pasta spirals
1/2 pound fresh broccoli
1/2 pound imitation crab meat
2 carrots, sliced
1 stalk celery, chopped
1 green bell pepper, chopped
1/4 cup oil
1/8 cup red wine vinegar
Thyme, rosemary, oregano and
   parsley to taste

Yield: 8 servings

Cook pasta using package directions; drain. Separate flowerets from broccoli stems. Pour boiling water over flowerets in colander; drain well. Combine broccoli, crab meat, carrots, celery and green pepper in large bowl; mix well. Combine oil and vinegar in small bowl. Add seasonings; mix well. Season with salt and pepper to taste. Pour over pasta. Chill until serving time. Serve on lettuce-lined plate.

Approx Per Serving: Cal 205; Prot 7.4 g; Carbo 28.2 g; T Fat 7.5 g; Chol 5.7 mg; Potas 474.0 mg; Sod 522.0 mg.

Melissa Marconi, New Jersey

SPAGHETTI SALAD

1 12-ounce package spaghetti
1/2 purple onion, chopped
2 tomatoes, chopped
2 cucumbers, sliced
1 green bell pepper, chopped
Salad Supreme seasoning
   to taste
1 8-ounce bottle of Viva
   Italian salad dressing

Yield: 10 servings

Cook spaghetti using package directions; drain. Place spaghetti in large bowl. Add onion, tomatoes, cucumbers, green pepper and Salad Supreme seasoning; mix well. Add salad dressing; toss to mix.

Approx Per Serving: Cal 164; Prot 2.2 g; Carbo 14.5 g; T Fat 14.0 g; Chol 0.0 mg; Potas 220.0 mg; Sod 116.0 mg.

Harrison Chapman, South Dakota

Rainbow Bean Salad

1 small bunch celery, finely
chopped
1 cucumber, chopped
1 onion, chopped
1 green bell pepper, chopped
1 red bell pepper, chopped
1 8-ounce can green beans
1 8-ounce can wax beans
1 8-ounce can peas, drained
4 tomatoes, coarsely chopped
1¹/₂ cups sugar
¹/₂ cup vinegar
¹/₂ cup oil
2 cups water

Yield: 20 servings

Combine celery, cucumber, onion, green pepper and red pepper in large bowl. Add water to cover. Let stand for 4 hours. Drain vegetables; rinse. Add drained beans, peas and tomatoes; mix well. Combine sugar, vinegar, oil and 2 cups water in large bowl; mix well. Pour over vegetable mixture. Marinate in refrigerator for 24 hours, stirring occasionally.

Approx Per Serving: Cal 132; Prot 1.3 g;
Carbo 20.7 g; T Fat 5.7 g; Chol 0.0 mg;
Potas 182.0 mg; Sod 93.0 mg.

Alicia Minton, Wisconsin

Fresh-Up Cabbage Salad

1¹/₂ teaspoons sugar
2 tablespoons vinegar
2 tablespoons oil
2 cups shredded cabbage
¹/₂ cup chopped parsley
1 medium onion, sliced into
rings

Yield: 8 servings

Combine sugar, vinegar and oil in small bowl; mix well. Combine cabbage, parsley and onion in bowl. Pour dressing over vegetables; toss to mix. Chill in refrigerator. Garnish with green pepper rings.

Approx Per Serving: Cal 46; Prot 0.5 g;
Carbo 3.7 g; T Fat 3.5 g; Chol 0.0 mg;
Potas 98.0; Sod 5.0 mg.

Sharon Kinley, Ohio

Cucumber and Yogurt Salad

3 cucumbers
1 tablespoon dried mint
1 cup plain yogurt

Yield: 8 servings

Peel cucumbers and slice very thin. Mix with mint and salt and pepper to taste in bowl. Add yogurt; mix gently. Chill for 1 hour.

Approx Per Serving: Cal 33; Prot 2.1 g;
Carbo 5.3 g; T Fat 0.6 g; Chol 1.8 mg;
Potas 234.0 mg; Sod 22.1 mg.

Willene Ryan, Tennessee

Mandarin Lettuce Salad

1 head lettuce, torn
1 11-ounce can mandarin
    oranges, drained
1/4 cup slivered almonds
2 tablespoons herbs and spices
    salad dressing

Yield: 8 servings

Combine lettuce, mandarin oranges and almonds in salad bowl; mix well. Add dressing; toss to mix.

Approx Per Serving: Cal 60; Prot 0.9 g; Carbo 7.6 g; T Fat 3.8 g; Chol 0.0 mg; Potas 74.6 mg; Sod 21.9 mg.

Elaine Hahn, Virginia

Juan de Salad

1 head romaine lettuce
1 cantaloupe, peeled, chopped
1/2 purple onion, chopped
1 tomato, chopped
1/4 cup olive oil
1/4 cup wine vinegar

Yield: 6 servings

Tear lettuce into bite-sized pieces; place in salad bowl. Add cantaloupe, onion and tomato; toss lightly. Drain well. Sprinkle with salt and pepper to taste. Pour olive oil and vinegar over salad; toss lightly.

Approx Per Serving: Cal 131; Prot 1.9 g; Carbo 11.8 g; T Fat 9.4 g; Chol 0.0 mg; Potas 477.0 mg; Sod 13.3 mg.

Pamela Marcos, New Mexico

Ever-Ready Slaw

1 large head cabbage, shredded
2 white onions, sliced
14 to 16 tablespoons sugar
3/4 cup oil
1 cup vinegar
2 teaspoons sugar
1 teaspoon dry mustard
1 teaspoon celery seed

Yield: 20 servings

Alternate 2 inch thick layers of cabbage with onions in bowl. Sprinkle 14 to 16 tablespoons sugar over top. Combine oil, vinegar, 2 teaspoons sugar, dry mustard and celery seed in saucepan. Bring to a full rolling boil. Pour over cabbage. Chill, loosely covered, for 4 hours. Mix well; spoon into covered jars. May store in refrigerator for several weeks.

Approx Per Serving: Cal 119; Prot 0.4 g; Carbo 12.1 g; T Fat 8.3 g; Chol 0.0 mg; Potas 78.7 mg; Sod 4.2 mg.

Karen Wagner, Mississippi

GREEN AND GOLD SALAD

1 cup chopped green bell
pepper
1 cup sliced celery
1/2 cup sliced green onions
2 tablespoons diced pimento
1   16-ounce can green beans
1   12-ounce can whole-kernel
corn, drained
1/2 cup sugar
1/2 teaspoon pepper
1/2 cup cider vinegar
1/4 cup oil

Yield: 10 servings

Combine green pepper, celery, onions, pimento, drained green beans and corn in large bowl. Mix sugar, pepper, vinegar and oil together in small bowl. Pour over salad; toss well. Chill, covered, for several hours or until serving time.

Approx Per Serving: Cal 131; Prot 1.7 g;
Carbo 20.5 g; T Fat 5.9 g; Chol 0.0 mg;
Potas 182.0 mg; Sod 204.4 mg.

Nancy Wittle, California

PICO DE GALLO

2 cups finely chopped, peeled
jicama
1 green bell pepper, slivered
1/2 medium onion, thinly sliced
1 cup chopped cucumber
1/4 cup olive oil
2 tablespoons vinegar
1/2 teaspoon oregano

Yield: 6 servings

Combine vegetables in bowl; mix gently. Combine olive oil, vinegar, oregano and salt and pepper to taste in small bowl; mix well. Pour over vegetables; toss to mix. Chill in refrigerator. Serve cold.

Approx Per Serving: Cal 110; Prot 0.9 g;
Carbo 7.0 g; T Fat 9.2 g; Chol 0.0 mg;
Potas 141.0 mg; Sod 21.6 mg.

Jeannie Wilson, Nebraska

GARDEN POTATO SALAD

2 pounds new red potatoes
1 cup (1-inch pieces) green
beans
1/2 cup canned corn
1/2 cup shredded carrots
1/4 cup plain yogurt
1/4 cup cottage cheese
2 teaspoons milk
1/2 teaspoon cider vinegar
1/2 teaspoon onion powder
1/4 teaspoon tarragon
1/8 teaspoon pepper

Yield: 8 servings

Cook potatoes in water to cover in saucepan until tender; drain. Rinse in cold water; drain. Cut potatoes into quarters. Cook green beans in 1-inch boiling water in saucepan for 2 to 3 minutes or until tender-crisp; drain. Combine potatoes, beans, corn and carrots in salad bowl. Combine remaining ingredients in blender container. Process at high speed until smooth. Pour over salad; mix lightly. Chill, covered, for 2 hours or longer.

Approx Per Serving: Cal 151; Prot 4.3 g;
Carbo 32.8 g; T Fat 0.8 g; Chol 2.1 mg;
Potas 559.0 mg; Sod 66.4 mg.

Etta Goins, Colorado

SPANISH SALAD

1/2 cup chopped onion
2 teaspoons minced garlic
2 teaspoons Dijon-style
mustard
1 teaspoon grated lemon rind
1/4 cup lemon juice
1/4 teaspoon oregano
1/4 teaspoon pepper
3/4 cup oil
1 cup soft bread crumbs
2 cups green pepper strips
3 cups shredded cabbage
2 cups chopped cucumber
4 cups chopped tomatoes
1 cup chopped celery
1/4 cup chopped parsley

Yield: 16 servings

Combine onion, garlic, mustard, lemon rind, lemon juice, oregano and pepper in blender container. Process until smooth. Add oil in fine stream, processing until creamy. Layer bread crumbs, green pepper, cabbage, cucumber, tomatoes, celery and dressing 1/2 at a time in 3-quart straight-sided glass dish. Chill, covered, for several hours. Sprinkle parsley over top.

Approx Per Serving: Cal 121; Prot 1.3 g;
Carbo 6.7 g; T Fat 10.6 g; Chol 0.0 mg;
Potas 231.0 mg; Sod 36.3 mg.

Neva Patterson, Montana

SUMMER SALAD

1 bunch broccoli, chopped
1 head cauliflower, chopped
2 cups sliced mushrooms
1   8-ounce can black olives
1 tablespoon chopped pimento
1   8-ounce bottle of oil-free
Italian dressing

Yield: 12 servings

Combine broccoli, cauliflower, mushrooms, olives and pimento in salad bowl. Add dressing; toss lightly.

Approx Per Serving: Cal 64; Prot 2.3 g;
Carbo 5.8 g; T Fat 5.2 g; Chol 1.1 mg;
Potas 308.0 mg; Sod 308.0 mg.

Clara Kupina, Georgia

FIRE AND ICE

6 large tomatoes
1 green pepper, cut into strips
1 medium onion, cut into rings
3/4 cup white vinegar
11/2 teaspoons cayenne pepper
11/2 teaspoons mustard seed
1/8 teaspoon pepper
1 tablespoon sugar
1/4 cup water
1 cucumber, peeled, sliced

Yield: 6 servings

Peel tomatoes and cut into quarters. Combine tomatoes, green pepper and onion in bowl. Combine vinegar, cayenne pepper, mustard seed, pepper, sugar and water in small saucepan. Bring to a boil. Cook for 1 minute. Pour over vegetables. Chill in refrigerator. Add cucumber just before serving.

Approx Per Serving: Cal 55; Prot 1.8 g;
Carbo 13.5 g; T Fat 0.5 g; Chol 0.0 mg;
Potas 434.0 mg; Sod 12.3 mg.

Vicki Jackson, Indiana

TOMATO AND CAULIFLOWER SALAD

2 3-ounce packages lemon
gelatin
2 cups boiling water
1½ cups cold water
3 tablespoons vinegar
⅛ teaspoon pepper
2 tablespoons finely chopped
green bell pepper
1 cup chopped tomatoes
3 tablespoons chopped onion
1 cup chopped cauliflower

Yield: 6 servings

Dissolve gelatin in boiling water in bowl. Add cold water, vinegar and pepper. Chill in refrigerator until partially set. Fold in green pepper, tomatoes, onion and cauliflower. Pour into oiled mold. Chill until firm. Unmold onto serving plate lined with salad greens. Serve with favorite salad dressing.

Approx Per Serving: Cal 118; Prot 3.3 g; Carbo 28.0 g; T Fat 0.1 g; Chol 0.0 mg; Potas 141.0 mg; Sod 94.7 mg.

Season Hubert, North Carolina

SAVORY TOFU MIX

1 pound tofu, drained, mashed
½ cup chopped green onions
½ cup grated carrots
½ cup soybean oil mayonnaise
2 tablespoons mustard
1 teaspoon garlic powder
¼ teaspoon turmeric

Yield: 6 servings

Combine tofu, green onions, carrots, mayonnaise, mustard, garlic powder and turmeric in bowl; mix well. Chill in refrigerator. Serve on bed of lettuce or as sandwich filling or dip.

Approx Per Serving: Cal 201; Prot 6.9 g; Carbo 4.0 g; T Fat 18.5 g; Chol 10.9 mg; Potas 161.0 mg; Sod 178.4 mg.

Paulette Gilbert, Nevada

ASPARAGUS SALAD DRESSING

1 16-ounce can cut asparagus
4 green onions, minced
½ cup mayonnaise
¼ cup lemon juice
Pepper to taste

Yield: 24 tablespoons

Drain asparagus, reserving 3 tablespoons juice. Mash asparagus with green onions in bowl. Add mayonnaise, lemon juice, reserved juice and pepper; mix well. Chill until serving time. Serve dressing over favorite green salad.

Approx Per Tablespoon: Cal 37; Prot 0.5 g; Carbo 1.1 g; T Fat 3.8 g; Chol 2.7 mg; Potas 46.7 mg; Sod 44.4 mg.

Julia Hardy, Arkansas

CAESAR SALAD DRESSING

1 can anchovies
1 cup light olive oil
1 egg
1 teaspoon dry mustard
1/2 cup Sherry vinegar
Garlic, Worcestershire sauce
and Tabasco sauce to taste

Yield: 32 tablespoons

Combine anchovies, oil, egg, dry mustard and vinegar in blender container; process until smooth. Add garlic, Worcestershire sauce and Tabasco sauce; mix well. Store in airtight container in refrigerator.

Approx Per Tablespoon: Cal 67; Prot 0.9 g; Carbo 0.2 g; T Fat 7.1 g; Chol 11.0 mg; Potas 19.4 mg; Sod 5.9 mg.

Clete Harvey, Washington

SWEET FRENCH DRESSING

1/4 cup orange juice
3/4 cup sugar
1 1/2 cups oil
1/2 cup vinegar
3/4 cup catsup
1 teaspoon celery seed
1 teaspoon paprika
2 teaspoons crushed dried parsley
1/8 teaspoon dry mustard
1/8 teaspoon pepper

Yield: 64 tablespoons

Process orange juice, sugar, oil, vinegar, catsup, celery seed, paprika, parsley, dry mustard and pepper in blender container until smooth. Serve with favorite salad.

Approx Per Tablespoon: Cal 58; Prot 0.1 g; Carbo 3.4 g; T Fat 5.1 g; Chol 0.0 mg; Potas 15.4 mg; Sod 33.7 mg.

Mary Lou Bean, Tennessee

ITALIAN DRESSING

1/3 cup oil
1/4 cup red wine vinegar
1/4 cup lemon juice
1 tablespoon sugar
1/2 teaspoon pepper
2 cloves of garlic, finely chopped

Yield: 16 tablespoons

Combine oil, vinegar, lemon juice, sugar, pepper and garlic in jar; shake well. Chill in refrigerator. Shake well before serving.

Approx Per Tablespoon: Cal 45; Prot 0.0 g; Carbo 1.5 g; T Fat 4.5 g; Chol 0.0 mg; Potas 10.1 mg; Sod 0.0 mg.

Sheila Mixson, Oklahoma

FLUFFY SALAD DRESSING

1½ tablespoons sugar
1 teaspoon mustard
½ teaspoon flour
¼ teaspoon cayenne pepper
2 teaspoons vinegar
2 egg yolks, beaten
¾ cup milk
1 tablespoon melted margarine
2 egg whites, stiffly beaten

Yield: 24 tablespoons

Combine sugar, mustard, flour and cayenne pepper in top of double boiler. Add vinegar and egg yolks; mix well. Stir in milk and margarine. Cook over hot water until thick and smooth, stirring frequently; remove from heat. Fold in egg whites gently. Cool. May make Thousand Island dressing by adding 2 tablespoons chopped sweet pickle, 2 tablespoons chopped green olives, 2 teaspoons chopped parsley and capers.

Approx Per Tablespoon: Cal 20; Prot 0.8 g; Carbo 1.5 g; T Fat 1.2 g; Chol 23.9 mg; Potas 21.2 mg; Sod 15.8 mg.

Grace Andersen, Minnesota

POPPY SEED DRESSING

3 tablespoons lemon juice
6 tablespoons tarragon vinegar
1 tablespoon grated onion
½ cup honey
½ cup sugar
2 teaspoons poppy seed
1 teaspoon dry mustard
1 teaspoon paprika
1 cup oil

Yield: 32 tablespoons

Combine lemon juice, vinegar, onion, honey, sugar, poppy seed and seasonings in blender container. Process until smooth. Add oil in fine stream, processing constantly. Store in airtight container in refrigerator. Serve over fruit salad.

Approx Per Tablespoon: Cal 89; Prot 0.0 g; Carbo 7.7 g; T Fat 6.8 g; Chol 0.0 mg; Potas 7.8 mg; Sod 0.3 mg.

Beatrice Riggins, Kentucky

SPECIAL THOUSAND ISLAND DRESSING

1 cup low-fat cottage cheese
½ cup chili sauce
1 teaspoon paprika
6 tablespoons skim milk
2 tablespoons finely chopped green bell pepper
2 hard-boiled eggs, chopped
2 tablespoons minced celery
1 tablespoon sweet pickle relish
1 tablespoon minced onion

Yield: 32 tablespoons

Combine cottage cheese, chili sauce, paprika and milk in blender container; process until smooth. Pour into bowl. Stir in green pepper, eggs, celery, pickle relish and onion. Chill in refrigerator.

Approx Per Tablespoon: Cal 18; Prot 1.6 g; Carbo 1.7 g; T Fat 0.5 g; Chol 17.8 mg; Potas 34.9 mg; Sod 95.7 mg.

Sue McCoy, Oklahoma

Main Dishes

MAIN DISHES

If you thought you'd have to give up all those hearty casseroles, rich-tasting meat dishes and heavenly sauces in the name of good nutrition, take heart—and hold on to those old family recipes.

Our chapter on Main Dishes will not only give you some fresh new recipes to try, but may inspire you to rewrite your own family's favorites in a more healthful light. Our basket of entrées includes dishes featuring meats, poultry and seafood, as well as meatless recipes that will please even the most resolute meat-and-potatoes man in your home.

In preparing entrées, there are a few cooking-light basics to keep in mind. With them you can modify almost any recipe and save calories, cholesterol, fat, sodium and sugar, while adding fiber and vitamins.

- Keep portions of red meat (beef, lamb, pork and veal) small (four or five uncooked ounces per serving). Avoid marbled cuts and look for lean cuts like flank steak, top or bottom round, tenderloin or trimmed sirloin. The center cuts of lamb or pork chops are the leanest.

- Try meatless meals more often, or use meat as an "accent" for pasta and vegetable dishes. Trimming visible fat from meat can cut fat and calories in half. Similarly, most of the fat in poultry can be found in the skin, so use skinless chicken or turkey pieces. Consider using low-fat ground turkey in place of ground beef, or turkey or chicken filets in place of beef or pork.

- Fish is low in fat and infinitely versatile, whether fresh or frozen. Try it baked, broiled or poached, seasoned with lemon juice, herbs and salt and pepper rather than butter or other oil. Water-packed canned fish contains a whopping 5 to 10 times less fat than oil-packed types.

- Do not deep-fry anything; there's just no healthy way to do this. Instead, try oven-frying, sparingly using low-fat margarine dotted on chicken or meat. When possible, substitute low-fat broths or other liquids for fat in recipes. Use butter sprinkles if a butter flavor is needed.

Once you've tried using these common-sense ideas in your meal preparation, they'll quickly become second nature. Cooking light isn't only a healthful alternative—it's a fresh, fun way to cook. And a great way to eat.

BEEF WITH PEA PODS

1 pound flank steak
4 ounces pea pods
1/4 cup oyster sauce
3 tablespoons sugar
3 cloves of garlic, crushed
1 1 1/2-inch piece gingerroot, crushed
1 teaspoon oil

Yield: 4 servings

Cut flank steak cross grain into 1/4-inch strips; cut into 3-inch pieces. Wash and string pea pods. Combine oyster sauce and sugar in small bowl; mix well. Heat wok on High. Add garlic, gingerroot and oil. Stir-fry for 30 seconds. Add pea pods. Stir-fry until pea pods are bright green; remove to bowl. Add steak. Stir-fry until no longer pink. Add pea pods and oyster sauce mixture. Stir-fry until heated through.

Approx Per Serving: Cal 237; Prot 20.9 g; Carbo 12.3 g; T Fat 11.1 g; Chol 63.8 mg; Potas 264.0 mg; Sod 35.7 mg. Nutritional information does not include oyster sauce.

Jeffrey Howard, California

CHUCK WAGON BEAN ROAST

1 3-pound chuck roast
1 pound pinto beans, rinsed
1 8-ounce can chopped green chilies
1 15-ounce can tomato sauce
1 8-ounce can Ro-Tel tomatoes and green chilies
1/4 teaspoon garlic salt
1 medium onion, thinly sliced

Yield: 16 servings

Place roast and beans in Dutch oven. Add water to cover, green chilies, tomato sauce, Ro-Tel tomatoes, garlic salt and onion. Bake, covered, at 250 degrees for 12 hours.

Approx Per Serving: Cal 277; Prot 17.7 g; Carbo 12.2 g; T Fat 17.6 g; Chol 58.0 mg; Potas 461.0 mg; Sod 243.0 mg.

Pauline Cheshier, Iowa

SPANISH STEAK

1 tablespoon dry mustard
1 2-pound round steak
3 tablespoons shortening
2 tablespoons chopped green bell pepper
1 tablespoon chopped onion
2 tablespoons chopped celery
2 cups chopped tomatoes
2 tablespoons chopped parsley
1 tablespoon Worcestershire sauce

Yield: 8 servings

Pound dry mustard into steak on both sides. Brown steak in hot shortening in skillet on both sides. Add green pepper, onion, celery, tomatoes, parsley, Worcestershire sauce and salt to taste; mix well. Place in 3-quart casserole. Cook, covered, at 350 degrees for 2 hours.

Approx Per Serving: Cal 269; Prot 20.5 g; Carbo 2.6 g; T Fat 19.2 g; Chol 65.4 mg; Potas 410.0 mg; Sod 71.0 mg.

Judith Curry, Illinois

SWISS STEAK

1½ pounds round steak
2 tablespoons flour
¼ teaspoon pepper
1 medium onion, chopped
2 8-ounce cans tomato sauce
1 tablespoon parsley flakes

Yield: 4 servings

Cut steak into serving-sized pieces. Combine flour and pepper on waxed paper. Pound flour mixture into steak with meat mallet. Place in 10-inch shallow dish. Sprinkle with onion. Pour tomato sauce over top. Sprinkle with parsley flakes. Microwave, covered, on High for 8 minutes. Microwave on Medium for 30 minutes or until tender. Let stand, covered, for 5 minutes.

Approx Per Serving: Cal 347; Prot 32.4 g; Carbo 14.2 g; T Fat 17.7 g; Chol 93.4 mg; Potas 893.0 mg; Sod 757.0 mg.

Andrea Cothren, Oklahoma

TOP ROUND STEAK WITH MUSHROOMS

1 tablespoon margarine
1 envelope dry onion soup mix
1½ pounds top round steak
1 tablespoon margarine
8 ounces mushrooms, sliced

Yield: 6 servings

Dot center of 2½-foot piece of heavy duty aluminum foil with 1 tablespoon margarine. Sprinkle half the onion soup mix over margarine. Place steak on prepared foil. Top with remaining onion soup mix, 1 tablespoon margarine and mushroom slices. Seal foil with double fold. Place on baking sheet. Bake at 300 degrees for 1¼ hours or until steak is tender. Serve with pan drippings.

Approx Per Serving: Cal 256; Prot 26.3 g; Carbo 12.6 g; T Fat 11.6 g; Chol 67.3 mg; Potas 607.0 mg; Sod 1779.0 mg.

Chance Alford, Alaska

SOUPER CASSEROLE

1 12-ounce package frozen noodles
8 cups boiling water
1 medium onion, chopped
¼ cup chopped celery
2 tablespoons shortening
1 pound ground beef
1 can cream of mushroom soup
1 can cream of chicken soup
¼ teaspoon pepper

Yield: 8 servings

Place noodles in boiling water; stir until separated. Simmer for 15 to 25 minutes or to desired degree of tenderness; drain. Sauté onion and celery in shortening in skillet until tender. Add ground beef. Cook until lightly browned, stirring constantly; drain. Add soups and pepper; mix well. Stir in noodles. Spoon into 9x13-inch casserole. Bake at 350 degrees for 20 minutes.

Approx Per Serving: Cal 272; Prot 13.0 g; Carbo 15.5 g; T Fat 17.4 g; Chol 51.1 mg; Potas 227.0 mg; Sod 646.5 mg.

Joan Robinson, Tennessee

SIX IN ONE

3/4 **pound ground beef**
1/2 **cup uncooked rice**
2 **potatoes, thinly sliced**
1 **onion, thinly sliced**
1 **green bell pepper, sliced**
1 **8-ounce can tomatoes**

Yield: 4 servings

Brown ground beef in skillet, stirring until crumbly; drain. Spoon into casserole. Layer rice, potatoes, onion, green pepper and tomatoes over ground beef. Bake at 350 degrees for 1 1/2 hours or until rice and vegetables are tender.

Approx Per Serving: Cal 208; Prot 18.7 g; Carbo 42.0 g; T Fat 13.4 g; Chol 54.8 mg; Potas 741.0 mg; Sod 149.5 mg.

Catherine Anderson, Wyoming

MEAT LOAF CASSEROLE

6 **carrots, sliced, cooked**
1 **10-ounce package frozen chopped broccoli, cooked**
1 **onion, chopped**
2 **stalks celery, chopped**
1/4 **teaspoon pepper**
2 1/2 **cups canned tomatoes**
1 **pound lean ground beef**
2 **cups bread crumbs**
2 **eggs, well beaten**
1 **cup chopped fresh parsley**

Yield: 12 servings

Combine carrots, broccoli, onion and celery in large bowl. Add pepper, tomatoes, ground beef, bread crumbs and eggs; mix well. Spoon into greased 3-quart casserole. Top with parsley. Bake at 300 degrees for 1 hour or until brown.

Approx Per Serving: Cal 216; Prot 12.6 g; Carbo 25.9 g; T Fat 7.5 g; Chol 71.2 mg; Potas 556.0 mg; Sod 314.3 mg.

Lois Webster, Indiana

CALIFORNIA CHILI

1 **pound ground beef**
1 **onion, chopped**
1/2 **green bell pepper, chopped**
1 **can tomato soup**
1 **cup catsup**
1 **15-ounce can kidney beans**
4 **cups cooked rice**

Yield: 8 servings

Brown ground beef with onion and green pepper in skillet, stirring until ground beef is crumbly; drain. Add soup and catsup; mix well. Heat through. Add beans, stirring gently. Cook until heated through. Serve over hot cooked rice.

Approx Per Serving: Cal 343; Prot 16.0 g; Carbo 48.2 g; T Fat 9.6 g; Chol 36.5 mg; Potas 532.0 mg; Sod 839.0 mg.

Milton Ryan, California

EASY CHILI

1 pound ground beef
1 small onion, chopped
1/4 teaspoon pepper
1 teaspoon chili powder
1/4 teaspoon paprika
1/4 teaspoon garlic powder
1/2 teaspoon red pepper
1/4 teaspoon cumin
1/4 cup catsup
1 cup tomato juice

Yield: 4 servings

Brown ground beef with onion in large skillet, stirring until ground beef is crumbly; drain. Add seasonings and catsup; mix well. Simmer for 10 minutes. Add tomato juice; mix well. Simmer for 15 minutes longer.

Approx Per Serving: Cal 278; Prot 20.5 g; Carbo 9.9 g; T Fat 17.3 g; Chol 73.0 mg; Potas 498.0 mg; Sod 466.0 mg.

Jennifer Godwin, New Jersey

CHEESE MEATBALLS

1 pound lean ground beef
8 ounces ground pork sausage
1 cup Parmesan cheese
1 cup milk
1 egg, beaten
1 cup crumbled bread
1/2 cup chopped parsley
1 large clove of garlic, minced
1/4 teaspoon pepper
1/4 cup margarine

Yield: 20 servings

Combine ground beef, sausage, cheese, milk, egg, bread, parsley, garlic and pepper in bowl; mix well. Shape into 48 meatballs. Brown in margarine in skillet over low heat; drain. Add to favorite spaghetti sauce. Simmer for several minutes. Serve over hot cooked spaghetti.

Approx Per Serving: Cal 164; Prot 8.6 g; Carbo 4.7 g; T Fat 12.2 g; Chol 42.9 mg; Potas 115.5 mg; Sod 229.4 mg.

Josephine Curtis, Michigan

SWEET AND SOUR MEATBALLS

2 slices bread
1/4 cup water
1 1/2 pounds ground beef
1/2 cup grated Parmesan cheese
1 egg, beaten
1 teaspoon chopped parsley
1 teaspoon basil
1/4 cup grated onion
1/4 cup finely chopped green bell pepper
1/2 cup grape jelly
1/2 cup chili sauce

Yield: 8 servings

Soak bread in water for several minutes; drain. Combine bread, ground beef, cheese, egg, parsley, basil, onion and green pepper in bowl; mix well. Shape into small meatballs. Combine grape jelly and chili sauce in saucepan; mix well. Bring to a boil. Add meatballs. Simmer for 30 minutes, stirring frequently. Skim surface.

Approx Per Serving: Cal 298; Prot 18.4 g; Carbo 21.3 g; T Fat 15.4 g; Chol 92.9 mg; Potas 300.0 mg; Sod 424.0 mg.

Patricia Spellman, California

MEAT LOAF

1½ pounds ground beef
¼ cup chopped onion
¼ cup chopped green bell
pepper
2 eggs, slightly beaten
½ cup oats
¼ cup Worcestershire sauce

Yield: 8 servings

Combine ground beef, onion, green pepper, eggs, oats and Worcestershire sauce in bowl; mix well. Pack into 4x8-inch loaf pan. Bake at 350 degrees for 1 hour. Drain. Cut into slices.

Approx Per Serving: Cal 293; Prot 22.6 g; Carbo 5.4 g; T Fat 19.6 g; Chol 145.0 mg; Potas 356.0 mg; Sod 161.0 mg.

Althea King, Kentucky

ZESTY MEAT LOAF

1½ pounds lean ground beef
4 ounces ground pork
¼ cup chopped onion
¼ cup catsup
1 cup oats
1 teaspoon salt
¼ teaspoon pepper
1 teaspoon mustard
1 egg, slightly beaten
1 cup milk
½ cup catsup

Yield: 8 servings

Combine ground beef, pork, onion, ¼ cup catsup, oats, salt, pepper, mustard, egg and milk in bowl; mix well. Press mixture into 8x12-inch baking dish. Spread with remaining ½ cup catsup. Bake at 375 degrees for 1 hour. Drain. Cool slightly before serving.

Approx Per Serving: Cal 303; Prot 22.6 g; Carbo 15.2 g; T Fat 16.9 g; Chol 104.0 mg; Potas 416.0 mg; Sod 619.5 mg.

Martha Shawn, Maryland

FRIED RICE

1 pound ground beef
¼ cup chopped green bell
pepper
¼ cup chopped onion
¾ cup cooked rice
2 tablespoons soy sauce

Yield: 6 servings

Brown ground beef in skillet just until pink. Add green pepper, onion and salt and pepper to taste; mix well. Cook, covered, until ground beef is cooked through; drain. Stir in rice and soy sauce. Cook for 5 minutes longer, adding water if necessary.

Approx Per Serving: Cal 191; Prot 13.7 g; Carbo 7.4 g; T Fat 11.5 g; Chol 48.7 mg; Potas 195.0 mg; Sod 388.0 mg.

Angela Custer, Idaho

HAMBURGER STEAK WITH SAVORY SAUCE

1½ pounds ground beef
Pepper to taste
¾ cup milk
¼ cup coffee
3 tablespoons catsup
2 tablespoons Worcestershire
sauce
4 slices bacon, crisp-fried,
crumbled

Yield: 6 servings

Combine first 3 ingredients in bowl; mix well. Shape into large patty. Place in skillet. Cook to desired degree of doneness. Drain excess drippings. Remove patty to platter. Add mixture of coffee, catsup and Worcestershire sauce to hot drippings. Heat until bubbly. Pour over ground beef steak. Sprinkle with bacon. Garnish with tomato wedges and parsley.

Approx Per Serving: Cal 291; Prot 21.8 g; Carbo 4.6 g; T Fat 20.2 g; Chol 80.7 mg; Potas 376.0 mg; Sod 285.7 mg.

Margarita Allen, New Mexico

SALISBURY STEAK

1 pound ground beef
1 tablespoon finely chopped
onion
¼ cup cracker crumbs
¼ teaspoon pepper
1 egg
1 can cream of mushroom soup
½ soup can water

Yield: 6 servings

Combine first 5 ingredints in bowl; mix well. Shape into 6 patties. Cook patties in skillet until brown on both sides. Arrange in greased 8x8-inch baking dish. Combine soup and water in bowl; mix well. Pour over patties. Bake at 350 degrees for 1 hour, turning patties once.

Approx Per Serving: Cal 239; Prot 15.2 g; Carbo 7.1 g; T Fat 16.4 g; Chol 95.2 mg; Potas 214.0 mg; Sod 498.7 mg.

Anthony Newman, Iowa

STUFFED PEPPERS

4 medium green bell peppers
3 cups boiling water
8 ounces ground beef
1   8-ounce can tomato sauce
1 cup cooked rice
¼ cup finely chopped celery
1 tablespoon instant minced
onion
2 teaspoons Worcestershire
sauce
1 teaspoon curry powder

Yield: 4 servings

Cut peppers into halves lengthwise, discarding seed. Place in boiling water in glass baking dish. Microwave on High for 4 to 5 minutes or until tender-crisp; drain. Crumble ground beef into small glass dish. Microwave on High until no longer pink; drain. Combine ground beef, tomato sauce, rice, celery, onion, Worcestershire sauce and curry powder in bowl; mix well. Spoon into pepper halves. Microwave, covered, on High for 30 minutes. Let stand for 5 minutes.

Approx Per Serving: Cal 341; Prot 22.2 g; Carbo 24.1 g; T Fat 17.8 g; Chol 73.0 mg; Potas 723.0 mg; Sod 446.0 mg.

Anita Carter, Oklahoma

CROCK·POT SPAGHETTI SAUCE

1 pound lean ground beef
1 large onion, chopped
1 clove of garlic, minced
2 16-ounce cans tomatoes, chopped
1 8-ounce can tomato sauce
1 12-ounce can tomato paste
1 cup beef bouillon
2 tablespoons minced parsley
1 tablespoon brown sugar
1 teaspoon oregano
1 teaspoon basil
1/4 teaspoon pepper

Yield: 6 servings

Brown ground beef with onion and garlic in skillet, stirring until ground beef is crumbly; drain. Spoon into Crock•Pot. Add tomatoes, tomato sauce, tomato paste, bouillon, parsley, brown sugar, oregano, basil and pepper; mix well. Cook, covered, on Low for 6 to 8 hours. Serve over hot cooked spaghetti.

Approx Per Serving: Cal 265; Prot 17.6 g; Carbo 23.8 g; T Fat 12.5 g; Chol 48.8 mg; Potas 1213.0 mg; Sod 657.7 mg.

Marie James, Missouri

ITALIAN SPAGHETTI SAUCE

12 ounces lean ground beef
12 ounces Italian sausage
1 tablespoon olive oil
1 onion, chopped
4 cloves of garlic, minced
3 bay leaves
1 tablespoon oregano
1 tablespoon sweet basil
2 teaspoons aniseed
2 tablespoons sugar
2 tablespoons Sherry
1 teaspoon barbecue seasoning
2 teaspoons Worcestershire sauce
1 tablespoon parsley flakes
1 28-ounce can whole tomatoes
1 28-ounce can tomato sauce
1 6-ounce can tomato paste

Yield: 12 servings

Sauté ground beef and sausage in olive oil in stockpot over high heat until meats begin to brown. Add onion and garlic. Sauté for 3 to 4 minutes or until onion is transparent; drain. Reduce heat. Add bay leaves, oregano, basil, aniseed, sugar, Sherry, barbecue seasoning, Worcestershire sauce, parsley flakes, tomatoes, tomato sauce, tomato paste and salt and pepper to taste; mix well. Simmer sauce for 1 to 1 1/2 hours, adding water if necessary for desired consistency. Remove bay leaves. Serve sauce over whole wheat spaghetti cooked *al dente* or vermicelli. Flavor improves if sauce is made a day ahead and reheated.

Approx Per Serving: Cal 196; Prot 11.6 g; Carbo 14.6 g; T Fat 10.7 g; Chol 34.0 mg; Potas 702.0 mg; Sod 726.0 mg.

Juanita Severa, California

SPAGHETTI BAKE

1 pound ground beef
1/2 cup chopped onion
1 16-ounce can tomatoes,
    drained
1 6-ounce can tomato paste
1 clove of garlic, minced
1/2 teaspoon oregano
1/2 teaspoon basil
1 7-ounce package spaghetti
2 cups milk
3 eggs, slightly beaten
Dash of pepper
1 cup Parmesan cheese
1 cup shredded mozzarella
    cheese

Yield: 15 servings

Brown ground beef with onion in skillet, stirring until ground beef is crumbly; drain. Stir in tomatoes, tomato paste, garlic, oregano and basil. Cook spaghetti according to package directions until just tender; drain. Spread in bottom of 9x13-inch baking dish. Combine milk, eggs and pepper in bowl; mix well. Pour over spaghetti. Sprinkle with Parmesan cheese. Spoon ground beef mixture over Parmesan cheese layer. Sprinkle with mozzarella cheese. Bake at 350 degrees for 40 to 45 minutes or until bubbly and cheese is melted.

Approx Per Serving: Cal 203; Prot 14.1 g; Carbo 10.1 g; T Fat 11.7 g; Chol 94.6 mg; Potas 329.0 mg; Sod 258.8 mg.

Maple Bizzell, Tennessee

CRANBERRY HAM

1 16-ounce can cranberry sauce
6 slices canned ham

Yield: 6 servings

Heat cranberry sauce in saucepan over medium heat until hot. Cut ham slices in half. Place in 7x11-inch baking dish, overlapping edges. Pour hot cranberry sauce over top. Bake, covered with foil, at 325 degrees until heated through. Do not overbake. Garnish with fresh orange slices.

Approx Per Serving: Cal 237; Prot 15.5 g; Carbo 29.5 g; T Fat 6.4 g; Chol 32.2 mg; Potas 304.0 mg; Sod 1107.0 mg.

Helen Gremley, Ohio

HAM STEW

2 cups 1 1/2-inch ham cubes
2 cups 1 1/2-inch yam cubes
1/2 cup packed brown sugar
2 tablespoons orange
    marmalade
1/4 teaspoon cloves
1 8-ounce can mixed
    vegetables

Yield: 6 servings

Combine ham, yams, brown sugar, marmalade, cloves and water to cover in 2-quart glass dish. Microwave on High for 10 minutes or until yams are tender. Stir in mixed vegetables.

Approx Per Serving: Cal 322; Prot 13.9 g; Carbo 35.3 g; T Fat 14.4 g; Chol 37.8 mg; Potas 582.0 mg; Sod 1101.0 mg.

Elva Adams, South Carolina

Spanish Lamb Stew

1 pound lean boneless lamb
1 large onion, sliced
1 green bell pepper
1 tablespoon olive oil
1 cup dry red wine
1 cup chopped tomatoes
1/4 cup golden raisins
1/4 cup chopped dried apricots
1 clove of garlic, minced
1/8 teaspoon pepper
1 teaspoon basil
1 teaspoon thyme
1 teaspoon tarragon
1 bay leaf
1/2 cup sliced mushrooms
1/4 cup sliced black olives
1 tablespoon flour
1 cup cold water

Yield: 6 servings

Cut lamb into 1-inch cubes. Slice onion 1/4-inch thick; cut green pepper into strips. Brown lamb in olive oil in large saucepan. Add wine, tomatoes, onion, green pepper, raisins, apricots, garlic, pepper and spices; mix well. Simmer, covered, for 1 hour. Add mushrooms and olives. Simmer for 30 minutes longer. Blend flour and water in small bowl. Stir into stew. Cook until thickened, stirring constantly. Remove bay leaf. Serve over white or brown rice or couscous.

Approx Per Serving: Cal 270; Prot 13.9 g; Carbo 16.0 g; T Fat 15.6 g; Chol 42.8 mg; Potas 503.0 mg; Sod 533.0 mg.

June McEwen, Kansas

Armenian Lamb Shanks

1 cup tomato juice
1/2 cup lemon juice
1/2 cup vinegar
1 onion, chopped
1 green bell pepper, chopped
1 teaspoon coarsely ground pepper
1 teaspoon cumin
1 teaspoon marjoram
6 lamb chops

Yield: 6 servings

Combine tomato juice, lemon juice, vinegar, onion, green pepper, pepper, cumin and marjoram in bowl; mix well. Add lamb chops. Marinate for 4 hours or longer. Place chops in roasting pan. Bake at 350 degrees for 1 hour or until tender.

Approx Per Serving: Cal 360; Prot 32.0 g; Carbo 7.5 g; T Fat 22.9 g; Chol 111.0 mg; Potas 594.0 mg; Sod 236.7 mg.
Nutritional information includes marinade.

Beatrice Reinhold, Florida

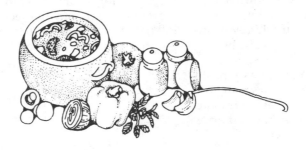

HONEY AND APPLE PORK CHOPS

1½ cups apple cider
¼ cup lemon juice
¼ cup soy sauce
2 tablespoons honey
1 clove of garlic, minced
¼ teaspoon pepper
4 2-ounce boneless pork chops

Yield: 4 servings

Combine first 6 ingredients in shallow dish; mix well. Add pork chops. Marinate, covered, in refrigerator overnight, turning chops occasionally. Drain, reserving marinade. Grill pork chops 6 inches from medium coals for 40 to 50 minutes, turning and basting frequently.

Approx Per Serving: Cal 253; Prot 16.0 g; Carbo 11.2 g; T Fat 15.9 g; Chol 58.3 mg; Potas 280.0 mg; Sod 554.0 mg.

Holly Hunt, Texas

PORK AND CARROT CASSEROLE

1½ pounds ground pork
¼ cup chopped onion
2 cups tomato sauce
⅛ teaspoon pepper
1 cup sour cream
1 cup cottage cheese
1 tablespoon parsley flakes
1 cup sliced carrots, cooked
1 8-ounce package noodles, cooked, drained
1 cup shredded Cheddar cheese

Yield: 15 servings

Brown ground pork with onion in skillet, stirring until ground pork is crumbly; drain. Stir in tomato sauce and pepper. Combine sour cream, cottage cheese, parsley and carrots in bowl; mix gently. Fold in noodles. Spread half the noodle mixture in 9x13-inch casserole. Spoon pork mixture over top. Spread remaining noodle mixture over pork layer. Sprinkle with cheese. Bake at 350 degrees for 30 minutes.

Approx Per Serving: Cal 261; Prot 15.3 g; Carbo 16.2 g; T Fat 14.9 g; Chol 52.5 mg; Potas 335.0 mg; Sod 344.5 mg.

Wilma Wright, Iowa

BARBECUED BEANS AND SAUSAGE

2 pounds Italian sausage
1 15-ounce can wax beans
1 15-ounce can green beans
1 15-ounce can pinto beans
1 15-ounce can lima beans
1 15-ounce can kidney beans
1 30-ounce can chili beans
1 can tomato soup
1 12-ounce can tomato paste
1 cup packed brown sugar
1 18-ounce jar barbecue sauce
1 18-ounce jar hot barbecue sauce

Yield: 30 servings

Crumble sausage into large skillet. Sauté until brown; drain. Drain canned wax, green, pinto, lima and kidney beans well. Stir in drained beans, chili beans, tomato soup, tomato paste, brown sugar and barbecue sauces. Pour into large casserole. Bake at 350 degrees for 1 hour or until flavors are blended.

Approx Per Serving: Cal 139; Prot 5.6 g; Carbo 27.7 g; T Fat 1.4 g; Chol 0.0 mg; Potas 449.0 mg; Sod 611.0 mg.

Dottie Van Gorder, Washington

SAUSAGE WITH RED BEANS AND RICE

1 pound dried red kidney beans
1 pound hot pork sausage,
sliced
1 onion, finely chopped
1 teaspoon (or more) garlic
1/2 teaspoon cayenne pepper
2 cups brown rice, cooked

Yield: 15 servings

Soak beans according to package directions; drain. Place in black iron pot with water to half the depth of beans. Add sausage, onion, garlic, pepper and salt to taste. Simmer, covered, for 2 hours or until beans are tender, stirring occasionally. Mash beans against side of pot with back of spoon to thicken. Add water if necessary. Simmer for 1 hour longer, stirring occasionally. Serve over hot rice.

Approx Per Serving: Cal 320; Prot 12.6 g;
Carbo 38.3 g; T Fat 13.0 g; Chol 20.7 mg;
Potas 558.8 mg; Sod 211.3 mg.

Steve Saunders, Kentucky

SAUSAGE AND EGG BAKE

2 pounds pork sausage
2 1/2 cups plain croutons
2 cups shredded Cheddar
cheese
5 eggs
3/4 teaspoon dry mustard
2 1/2 cups milk
1 can cream of mushroom soup
1/2 cup milk

Yield: 15 servings

Cook sausage in skillet until brown, stirring until crumbly; drain well. Layer croutons, cheese and sausage in greased 9x13-inch baking dish. Beat eggs with dry mustard and 2 1/2 cups milk; pour over layers. Chill, covered, in refrigerator for several hours to overnight. Mix soup and 1/2 cup milk in small bowl; spoon over top. Bake at 325 degrees for 1 hour. Let stand for 10 to 15 minutes before cutting.

Approx Per Serving: Cal 407; Prot 15.4 g;
Carbo 8.3 g; T Fat 34.5 g; Chol 155.0 mg;
Potas 246.0 mg; Sod 760.0 mg.

Henrietta Hoff, South Dakota

SAUSAGES WITH PEPPERS AND ONIONS

1 1/2 pounds sweet or hot Italian
sausages
2 tablespoons olive oil
3 large onions, slivered
4 cloves of garlic, minced
3 red bell peppers
3 green bell peppers
3 yellow bell peppers
1/2 teaspoon oregano
1/2 teaspoon Italian parsley

Yield: 6 servings

Brown sausages in 1 tablespoon olive oil in skillet over medium-low heat. Add remaining 1 tablespoon olive oil, onions and garlic. Cook until onions are tender. Slice peppers into strips. Stir peppers, oregano and parsley into skillet. Cook until peppers are tender.

Approx Per Serving: Cal 277; Prot 13.0 g;
Carbo 15.4 g; T Fat 19.0 g; Chol 41.1 mg;
Potas 590.0 mg; Sod 496.0 mg.

Luis Alvarado, California

VENISON CURRY

1/4 cup chopped onion
1 teaspoon garlic flakes
2 tablespoons oil
1 pound thinly sliced venison,
cut into 1-inch strips
1/4 teaspoon ginger
1 teaspoon curry powder
1 tablespoon soy sauce
1 cup beef bouillon stock
1/2 teaspoon sugar
1 tablespoon lemon juice
1 tablespoon cornstarch
1 tablespoon water

Yield: 5 servings

Sauté onion and garlic in oil in large skillet until tender, stirring constantly. Add venison. Cook until brown, stirring frequently. Combine next 6 ingredients in bowl; mix with wire whisk. Add to venison. Simmer, covered, for 20 minutes. Blend cornstarch and water in bowl with wire whisk. Add to venison gradually, stirring constantly. Cook until mixture thickens, stirring constantly. Serve over rice.

Approx Per Serving: Cal 163; Prot 20.9 g;
Carbo 3.0 g; T Fat 7.1 g; Chol 44.3 mg;
Potas 277.0 mg; Sod 410.0 mg.

Marybell Mann, Maryland

VENISON STEW

3 pounds boneless venison,
cubed
1/2 cup vinegar
2 cloves of garlic, minced
2 cups cold water
2 tablespoons oil
1 cup chopped onion
1/3 cup chopped green bell
pepper
1 cup sliced celery
1/2 teaspoon oregano
1 tablespoon dried parsley
1 cup tomato juice or apple
cider
3 tablespoons catsup
Pepper to taste

Yield: 10 servings

Place venison in plastic bag in large bowl. Combine vinegar and garlic; pour over venison. Add enough water to cover. Seal bag. Marinate overnight. Drain. Sauté venison in oil in skillet until brown, stirring constantly. Remove from heat. Combine vegetables and seasonings in Crock•Pot; mix well. Add venison, tomato juice and catsup; mix well. Cook on High for 4 to 5 hours. Cook on Low for 8 to 12 hours. Season with salt and pepper to taste.

Approx Per Serving: Cal 193; Prot 30.7 g;
Carbo 5.0 g; T Fat 5.1 g; Chol 66.3 mg;
Potas 495.0 mg; Sod 224.0 mg.

Peggy Richardson, North Carolina

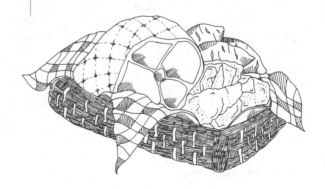

CHICKEN CHOW MEIN

2 cups drained bean sprouts
2 cups chopped mushrooms
1 cup water
1/4 cup onion flakes
4 envelopes chicken broth and
seasoning mix
1 teaspoon garlic powder
1　8-ounce can sliced water
chestnuts
16 ounces cooked chicken,
finely chopped

Yield: 4 servings

Combine all ingredients except chicken in saucepan; mix well. Simmer for 5 minutes. Stir in chicken. Cook until heated through. Serve over chow mein noodles.

Approx Per Serving: Cal 272; Prot 35.8 g;
Carbo 12.6 g; T Fat 8.7 g; Chol 101.0 mg;
Potas 565.0 mg; Sod 156.0 mg.

Gladys Shamley, Maine

CHICKEN DIJON

4 chicken breast filets
3 tablespoons margarine
2 tablespoons flour
1 cup chicken broth
1/2 cup half and half
2 tablespoons Dijon mustard

Yield: 4 servings

Sauté chicken breasts in margarine in skillet for 20 minutes. Remove to warm platter; keep warm. Stir flour into pan drippings. Add broth and half and half. Simmer until thickened, stirring constantly. Add mustard; mix well. Return chicken breasts to skillet. Heat, covered, for 10 minutes.

Approx Per Serving: Cal 287; Prot 28.8 g;
Carbo 4.8 g; T Fat 16.4 g; Chol 82.8 mg;
Potas 298.0 mg; Sod 440.0 mg.

Pat Segal, Maryland

OVEN-FRIED CHICKEN

1 1/2 cups bran flakes cereal
1/2 teaspoon garlic powder
1/2 teaspoon oregano
1/8 teaspoon pepper
2 tablespoons oil
4 chicken breast filets

Yield: 4 servings

Combine cereal, garlic powder, oregano and pepper in blender container; process until cereal is finely crushed. Place in bowl. Add oil; mix until crumbs are moist. Dip chicken into water; coat with cereal mixture. Place in baking dish. Bake at 400 degrees for 20 to 25 minutes or until crisp and brown.

Approx Per Serving: Cal 254; Prot 28.1 g;
Carbo 11.4 g; T Fat 10.9 g; Chol 71.7 mg;
Potas 303.0 mg; Sod 202.0 mg.

Joyce Geddes, Mississippi

GRILLED CHICKEN

1/2 cup oil
1 cup vinegar
1 teaspoon salt
1/4 teaspoon pepper
1 1/2 teaspoons poultry
seasoning
1 egg
2 whole chickens, cut up

Yield: 8 servings

Combine oil, vinegar, salt, pepper, poultry seasoning and egg in blender container; process until smooth. Grill chicken for 45 minutes or until chicken is tender, turning and basting with oil mixture frequently.

Approx Per Serving: Cal 296; Prot 25.3 g; Carbo 2.0 g; T Fat 21.0 g; Chol 110.0 mg; Potas 247.0 mg; Sod 373.5 mg.

Joan Heinsohn, Arizona

LEMON MINT CHICKEN

4 chicken breasts
1/4 cup fresh lemon juice
2 teaspoons chopped fresh mint
3 cloves of garlic, crushed
1 cup plain yogurt
1/4 teaspoon (or less) red pepper

Yield: 4 servings

Rinse chicken and pat dry. Combine lemon juice, mint, garlic, yogurt and red pepper in bowl. Add chicken. Marinate in refrigerator for 1 hour to overnight. Drain marinade. Grill over coals or broil in oven for 20 minutes or until tender.

Approx Per Serving: Cal 209; Prot 27.5 g; Carbo 4.7 g; T Fat 8.5 g; Chol 79.4 mg; Potas 324.0 mg; Sod 86.0 mg.

Miller Bevan, Louisiana

CHICKEN ENCHILADA

1 small onion, chopped
1 tablespoon oil
2 8-ounce cans tomato sauce
1/4 cup water
1 tablespoon chili powder
12 corn tortillas
3 cups chopped cooked chicken
3 cups shredded Cheddar
cheese

Yield: 12 servings

Sauté onion in oil in saucepan. Add tomato sauce, water and chili powder. Simmer for 20 minutes. Dip tortillas 1 at a time in sauce. Place chicken on tortillas. Roll to enclose chicken. Place in baking dish. Top with cheese and remaining sauce. Bake at 350 degrees just until cheese is melted. Serve immediately.

Approx Per Serving: Cal 242; Prot 18.8 g; Carbo 11.3 g; T Fat 13.8 g; Chol 61.0 mg; Potas 293.0 mg; Sod 434.3 mg.

Rose Reyes, Texas

LOW-CHOLESTEROL MEXICAN CHICKEN

1 medium onion, chopped
1 teaspoon chili powder
1/2 teaspoon garlic powder
8 ounces imitation cheese, shredded
1 10-ounce can tomatoes and green chilies, mashed
1 3-pound chicken, cooked, chopped
2 cans cream of chicken soup
10 corn tortillas

Yield: 12 servings

Combine onion, chili powder, garlic powder, cheese, tomatoes and green chilies and chicken in bowl; mix well. Heat soup in saucepan. Dip tortillas into soup to soften. Line baking dish with tortillas; top with chicken mixture. Pour remaining soup over all. Bake at 350 degrees for 35 minutes or until hot and bubbly.

Approx Per Serving: Cal 332; Prot 29.8 g; Carbo 18.9 g; T Fat 15.4 g; Chol 89.2 mg; Potas 367.0 mg; Sod 728.0 mg.

Rita Childress, New Hampshire

MICROWAVE ORANGE CHICKEN WITH LEMON PEPPER

4 chicken breast filets
1 tablespoon Parmesan cheese
1 tablespoon chopped fresh parsley
2 teaspoons grated orange rind
1/4 cup orange juice
1 tablespoon dry white wine
1 teaspoon lemon juice
Sections of 4 medium oranges
2 teaspoons lemon pepper

Yield: 4 servings

Arrange chicken filets around outer edge of 9-inch glass pie plate. Sprinkle with cheese, parsley and orange rind; drizzle with orange juice, wine and lemon juice. Microwave, tightly covered, on High for 4 minutes. Turn chicken filets; arrange orange sections in center of pie plate. Microwave, tightly covered, for 2 to 6 minutes longer or until chicken is tender. Place on serving platter; drizzle with pan drippings. Sprinkle with lemon pepper.

Approx Per Serving: Cal 224; Prot 28.2 g; Carbo 17.5 g; T Fat 4.4 g; Chol 72.7 mg; Potas 490.0 mg; Sod 90.1 mg.

Marion Strong, Idaho

RUSSIAN CHICKEN

8 chicken breast filets
2 tablespoons flour
1/8 teaspoon pepper
1 20-ounce can chunk pineapple, drained
1 8-ounce bottle of Russian salad dressing

Yield: 8 servings

Coat chicken breast filets with mixture of flour and pepper. Arrange in 8x10-inch baking dish. Spoon pineapple over chicken. Pour salad dressing over top. Bake at 325 degrees for 1 hour or until chicken is tender. May use reduced calorie salad dressing.

Approx Per Serving: Cal 265; Prot 18.3 g; Carbo 18.1 g; T Fat 13.5 g; Chol 61.6 mg; Potas 249.0 mg; Sod 228.8 mg.

Leslie Cooper, Virginia

CHICKEN POTPIE

1 cup low-sodium chicken
broth
1/4 cup chopped onion
1 tablespoon cornstarch
1/2 cup cold skim milk
1/8 teaspoon pepper
2 tablespoons chopped parsley
1 cup finely chopped cooked
chicken
1/2 cup finely chopped cooked
potato
1/2 cup finely chopped cooked
carrot
1 5-ounce can corn
1 cup bran flakes, crushed
1 tablespoon oil
1/2 teaspoon marjoram
1/2 teaspoon tarragon
1/2 teaspoon oregano

Yield: 4 servings

Combine chicken broth and onion in saucepan. Mix cornstarch with milk in small bowl. Stir into broth gradually. Cook over medium heat until thickened, stirring constantly. Stir in pepper and parsley. Layer chicken, potato, carrot and corn in 1-quart casserole. Spoon broth mixture over layers. Combine bran flakes, oil and seasonings in small bowl; mix well. Sprinkle over casserole. Bake at 350 degrees for 30 minutes or until hot and bubbly.

Approx Per Serving: Cal 204; Prot 14.1 g;
Carbo 24.4 g; T Fat 6.7 g; Chol 31.7 mg;
Potas 383.0 mg; Sod 242.0 mg.

Phillis Graves, Oklahoma

SPINACH-STUFFED CHICKEN BREASTS

1/4 cup chopped onion
2 tablespoons oil
1 10-ounce package frozen
chopped spinach, cooked,
drained
3 ounces cream cheese
1/2 cup bread crumbs
1/4 teaspoon garlic salt
6 chicken breasts
1/4 cup honey
1 teaspoon melted margarine
2 teaspoons lemon juice
2 teaspoons prepared mustard

Yield: 6 servings

Sauté onion in oil in skillet for 5 minutes. Add spinach. Sauté 2 minutes longer. Add cream cheese, bread crumbs and garlic salt. Cook until cream cheese melts. Arrange chicken breasts in 9x13-inch casserole. Spoon stuffing mixture under skin of each chicken breast. Baste with mixture of honey, margarine, lemon juice and prepared mustard. Bake at 350 degrees for 45 to 60 minutes or until chicken is brown.

Approx Per Serving: Cal 334; Prot 30.1 g;
Carbo 21.2 g; T Fat 14.6 g; Chol 87.6 mg;
Potas 400.0 mg; Sod 417.0 mg.

Tom Hollander, Washington, D.C.

Hot Chicken Salad

4 cups chopped cooked chicken
2 cups chopped celery
1/2 teaspoon pepper
1 tablespoon minced onion
3 tablespoons lemon juice
1/2 cup mayonnaise
1 can cream of chicken soup
1 cup cooked rice
1/2 cup crushed pineapple
1   8-ounce can sliced water
    chestnuts, drained
1 1/2 cups crushed potato chips
1/2 cup shredded Cheddar
    cheese

Yield: 12 servings

Combine chicken, celery, pepper, onion, lemon juice, mayonnaise, soup, rice, pineapple and water chestnuts in bowl; mix well. Spoon into 9x13-inch baking dish. Sprinkle potato chips and cheese over top. Bake at 325 degrees for 30 to 40 minutes or until hot and bubbly.

Approx Per Serving: Cal 257; Prot 16.4 g; Carbo 14.1 g; T Fat 15.2 g; Chol 54.1 mg; Potas 290.0 mg; Sod 358.3 mg.

Richmond Everly, Wisconsin

Brunswick Stew

2 1/2 to 3 pounds chicken
2 stalks celery
1 small onion
4 cups water
2 quarts tomatoes
3 medium potatoes, peeled
1 cup chopped onion
4 cups drained green butter
    beans
4 cups drained whole kernel
    corn
5 tablespoons sugar
Red and black pepper to taste

Yield: 16 servings

Wash chicken and pat dry. Combine with celery, small onion and water in 8-quart stockpot. Simmer until chicken is tender. Remove chicken; bone and chop. Strain cooled broth. Combine broth, tomatoes, whole potatoes and chopped onion in stockpot. Cook over medium heat until potatoes are tender. Remove potatoes and chop. Add chopped potatoes, chicken, butter beans, corn and sugar to stew. Season with salt and red and black pepper to taste. Simmer, covered, for 3 to 5 hours or until tomatoes have cooked to pieces, stirring occasionally. Mash potatoes rather than chopping if stew is to be frozen.

Approx Per Serving: Cal 295; Prot 29.6 g; Carbo 29.0 g; T Fat 7.2 g; Chol 75.9 mg; Potas 708.0 mg; Sod 193.0 mg.

Herbert Brock, Kentucky

STIR-FRIED CHICKEN

1/4 cup soy sauce
1/4 teaspoon garlic powder
2 teaspoons cornstarch
1 cup uncooked sliced chicken
1 cup chicken broth
1/4 teaspoon ginger
2 tablespoons cornstarch
2 tablespoons soy sauce
1/4 teaspoon garlic powder
2 tablespoons oil
1 cup thinly sliced celery
1/2 cup thinly sliced carrots
1/2 cup thinly sliced onion
1/2 cup fresh pea pods
1/2 cup thinly sliced mushrooms
1 cup fresh bean sprouts

Yield: 4 servings

Combine 1/4 cup soy sauce, 1/4 teaspoon garlic powder and 2 teaspoons cornstarch in bowl; mix well. Add chicken. Let stand for several minutes; drain. Combine broth, ginger, 2 tablespoons cornstarch, 2 tablespoons soy sauce and 1/4 teaspoon garlic powder in small bowl; mix well. Heat oil in wok. Add marinated chicken. Stir-fry until slightly brown. Remove from wok. Stir-fry celery, carrots and onion in wok until tender-crisp. Add pea pods, mushrooms, bean sprouts and cooked chicken. Pour in broth mixture. Cook until thickened, stirring occasionally. Add additional broth if necessary.

Approx Per Serving: Cal 192; Prot 12.4 g; Carbo 15.4 g; T Fat 9.4 g; Chol 23.7 mg; Potas 437.0 mg; Sod 484.0 mg.

George Augustus, Utah

ORANGE-GLAZED CHICKEN AND VEGETABLES

2 tablespoons flour
1/2 teaspoon paprika
1/8 teaspoon pepper
4 chicken breasts, boned, skinned
1 tablespoon oil
1/4 cup orange juice
1/4 cup orange marmalade
1 16-ounce can whole baby carrots, drained
1 10-ounce package frozen peas and onions
1 tablespoon orange marmalade

Yield: 5 servings

Combine flour, paprika and pepper in shallow 10-inch dish. Coat chicken with flour mixture. Brown chicken for 3 minutes on each side in oil in skillet. Combine orange juice and 1/4 cup marmalade in bowl. Pour over chicken. Cook for 6 minutes. Remove chicken to warm platter. Add carrots, peas and onions to pan drippings in skillet. Arrange chicken on top. Spread with remaining 1 tablespoon marmalade. Simmer, covered, over medium heat for 5 minutes longer.

Approx Per Serving: Cal 276; Prot 24.9 g; Carbo 30.8 g; T Fat 6.1 g; Chol 57.3 mg; Potas 478.0 mg; Sod 459.8 mg.

Mary Holcombe, Maryland

Turkey Oven Barbecue

2 large turkey drumsticks
1 cup water
1 small onion, chopped
1/2 cup catsup
1/3 cup maple syrup
1 1/2 teaspoons dry mustard

Yield: 4 servings

Rinse drumsticks; pat dry. Combine with water in 2-quart casserole. Bake, covered, at 350 degrees for 2 hours; drain. Mix onion, catsup, syrup and dry mustard in small bowl. Pour over turkey. Bake, uncovered, for 30 minutes longer.

Approx Per Serving: Cal 218; Prot 17.2 g; Carbo 27.7 g; T Fat 4.3 g; Chol 48.2 mg; Potas 369.0 mg; Sod 405.0 mg.

Jennifer Lewellewyn, California

Turkey Casserole

2 cans cream of chicken soup
1 cup mayonnaise-type salad dressing
1 teaspoon (rounded) curry powder
1 6-ounce can sliced mushrooms
1 1/2 tablespoons lemon juice
2 10-ounce packages frozen broccoli, cooked
2 cups cooked chopped turkey
1 cup shredded Cheddar cheese

Yield: 8 servings

Combine soup, salad dressing, curry powder, mushrooms and lemon juice in bowl; mix well. Add broccoli and turkey; mix well. Pour into 9x13-inch baking dish. Top with cheese. Bake at 350 degrees for 30 minutes. May use low salt soup to reduce sodium.

Approx Per Serving: Cal 327; Prot 19.0 g; Carbo 18.0 g; T Fat 21.0 g; Chol 55.0 mg; Potas 336.0 mg; Sod 1027.0 mg.

Naomi Weiss, Illinois

Easy Turkey Chili

2 pounds ground turkey
1 ounce chili powder
4 8-ounce cans tomato sauce
1/2 teaspoon cayenne pepper
1 cup water

Yield: 12 servings

Brown ground turkey in large skillet, stirring until crumbly; drain. Add chili powder, tomato sauce, cayenne pepper and water. Simmer for 15 minutes, stirring occasionally and adding water as needed. Adjust seasonings to taste. May add 1/4 cup masa corn mix mixed with a small amount of hot water and 2 cups chili beans.

Approx Per Serving: Cal 150; Prot 15.7 g; Carbo 5.4 g; T Fat 7.5 g; Chol 47.6 mg; Potas 414.0 mg; Sod 522.0 mg.

Lawrence Williams, Vermont

TEXICAN CHILI

10 ounces ground turkey
1 16-ounce can brown beans
1¼ cups tomato sauce
½ cup chopped onion
¼ cup chopped celery
1 clove of garlic, minced
1 tablespoon chili powder
¼ teaspoon cumin
2 cups canned tomatoes, drained
¼ cup chopped green bell pepper
½ cup thinly sliced carrot
⅛ teaspoon pepper

Yield: 6 servings

Brown ground turkey in large saucepan, stirring until crumbly; drain. Add beans, tomato sauce, onion, celery, garlic, chili powder, cumin, tomatoes, green pepper, carrot and pepper. Cook over low heat for 2 hours, stirring frequently.

Approx Per Serving: Cal 213; Prot 17.0 g; Carbo 26.8 g; T Fat 5.0 g; Chol 27.8 mg; Potas 823.0 mg; Sod 486.3 mg.

Virginia Combs, Missouri

TURKEY DELIGHT

1 cup cooked rice
1 can cream of celery soup
2 tablespoons chopped onion
2 tablespoons chopped pimento
½ cup mayonnaise
2 cups cooked chopped turkey
2 cups French-style green beans
1 cup water chestnuts

Yield: 8 servings

Combine rice, soup, onion, pimento and mayonnaise in 2-quart casserole; mix well. Add turkey, green beans, water chestnuts and salt and pepper to taste; mix lightly. Bake at 350 degrees for 50 minutes.

Approx Per Serving: Cal 229; Prot 12.0 g; Carbo 13.2 g; T Fat 14.5 g; Chol 39.1 mg; Potas 212.0 mg; Sod 477.0 mg.

Jacqueline Green, Arkansas

STIR-FRY TURKEY

8 ounces ground turkey
1 tablespoon oil
1 carrot, sliced
1 stalk celery, sliced
½ cup sliced green bell pepper
½ cup sliced mushrooms
½ cup sliced water chestnuts
3 tablespoons soy sauce
1 tablespoon cornstarch
1 teaspoon sugar

Yield: 4 servings

Brown ground turkey in oil in skillet, stirring frequently. Add vegetables. Stir-fry until tender-crisp. Stir in mixture of soy sauce, cornstarch and sugar. Cook until heated through, stirring constantly. Serve over rice. May substitute broccoli, bean sprouts, green onions or other vegetables of choice for vegetables listed.

Approx Per Serving: Cal 207; Prot 16.2 g; Carbo 10.9 g; T Fat 11.0 g; Chol 47.6 mg; Potas 392.0 mg; Sod 855.0 mg.

Chris Mack, Washington

CLAM LINGUINE

5 cloves of garlic, minced
1/4 cup olive oil
3 7-ounce cans minced clams
1/2 cup dry white wine
1/2 cup clam juice
1/2 cup chopped fresh parsley
1 teaspoon basil
1 teaspoon oregano
1 teaspoon pepper
1 8-ounce package linguine, cooked

Yield: 4 servings

Sauté garlic in olive oil in large skillet. Add clams, wine, clam juice, parsley, basil, oregano and pepper; mix well. Heat mixture to serving temperature. Pour over hot linguine. Garnish with Parmesan cheese.

Approx Per Serving: Cal 289; Prot 14.3 g; Carbo 19.5 g; T Fat 24.3 g; Chol 93.8 mg; Potas 333.0 mg; Sod 68.3 mg.

Joy Rickey, New York

DEVILED CRAB AND CORN

1/4 cup margarine
2 tablespoons flour
1 teaspoon prepared mustard
1 tablespoon lemon juice
1/2 teaspoon Worcestershire sauce
Dash of pepper
1/2 cup milk
2 hard-boiled eggs, chopped
1 6-ounce package frozen crab meat, thawed
1 16-ounce can whole kernel corn, drained
1 16-ounce can cream-style corn
1/2 cup Parmesan cheese
1/2 cup coarse cracker crumbs
1 tablespoon melted margarine

Yield: 6 servings

Melt 1/4 cup margarine in saucepan. Stir in flour, mustard, lemon juice, Worcestershire sauce and pepper. Add milk; mix well. Cook until thickened and bubbly, stirring constantly. Remove from heat. Stir in eggs, crab meat, whole kernel corn and cream-style corn gently. Spoon into 1 1/2-quart casserole. Sprinkle with Parmesan cheese. Top with mixture of cracker crumbs and 1 tablespoon melted margarine. Bake at 350 degrees for 45 minutes or until heated through. Garnish casserole with hard-boiled egg wedges and olive slices.

Approx Per Serving: Cal 337; Prot 14.6 g; Carbo 37.4 g; T Fat 16.5 g; Chol 120.2 mg; Potas 428.0 mg; Sod 1276.0 mg.

Libby Newcomb, Tennessee

IMPERIAL CRAB

2 eggs, well beaten
1 pound back-fin crab meat
Dash of red pepper
1 green bell pepper, diced
1/4 cup mayonnaise
1 tablespoon chopped onion
1 tablespoon mayonnaise

Yield: 6 servings

Reserve 2 tablespoons beaten egg. Combine crab meat, salt to taste, red pepper, green pepper, remaining beaten eggs, 1/4 cup mayonnaise and onion in bowl; mix well. Spoon crab mixture into individual ramekins or baking shells. Combine remaining 1 tablespoon mayonnaise and reserved 2 tablespoons egg in bowl; mix well. Spoon over crab meat. Sprinkle with red pepper to taste. Bake at 350 degrees for 30 minutes or until heated through.

Approx Per Serving: Cal 190; Prot 17.6 g; Carbo 1.5 g; T Fat 12.4 g; Chol 174.0 mg; Potas 306.0 mg; Sod 299.0 mg.

Tom Wilson, Maryland

SCALLOPS SAINT JACQUES

1/4 cup margarine
3 tablespoons flour
1/4 teaspoon dry mustard
1/2 teaspoon grated lemon rind
1/2 teaspoon powdered
horseradish
2 cups half and half
1 1/2 cups sliced mushrooms
2 teaspoons instant onion
flakes
2 tablespoons margarine
8 ounces scallops
8 ounces shrimp, peeled,
cooked
4 ounces crab meat
2 tablespoons dry Sherry
1/4 cup bread crumbs

Yield: 10 servings

Melt 1/4 cup margarine in saucepan. Stir in flour, dry mustard, lemon rind and horseradish. Add half and half. Cook until thickened, stirring constantly. Sauté mushrooms and onion flakes in 2 tablespoons margarine in skillet. Remove to sauce with slotted spoon. Cut scallops into bite-sized pieces. Add to skillet. Sauté for 3 minutes. Add scallops to sauce with shrimp, crab meat and Sherry; mix well. Spoon into individual shells or ramekins. Top with bread crumbs. Bake at 400 degrees for 10 minutes. Broil just until light brown.

Approx Per Serving: Cal 198; Prot 12.8 g; Carbo 5.9 g; T Fat 13.3 g; Chol 71.1 mg; Potas 265.0 mg; Sod 350.0 mg.

Joan McDermott, Colorado

SCAMPI

³/4 pound medium shrimp
1 tablespoon chopped green
onions
6 tablespoons margarine
1 tablespoon olive oil
4 cloves of garlic, minced
2 teaspoons lemon juice
2 tablespoons minced parsley
¹/8 teaspoon Tabasco sauce
¹/4 teaspoon lemon rind

Yield: 4 servings

Peel and devein shrimp. Sauté green onions in margarine and olive oil in skillet with garlic and lemon juice until bubbly. Add shrimp. Cook for 4 minutes or until shrimp are pink, stirring occasionally. Stir in parsley, Tabasco sauce and lemon rind.

Approx Per Serving: Cal 275; Prot 18.4 g; Carbo 2.0 g; T Fat 21.6 g; Chol 166.0 mg; Potas 219.0 mg; Sod 338.0 mg.

Heather Long, California

EASY EASY SHRIMP CREOLE

1 medium onion, chopped
1 small green bell pepper,
chopped
2 tablespoons olive oil
1 8-ounce can tomato sauce
1 10-ounce can Ro-Tel
tomatoes
1 teaspoon minced garlic
1 pound shrimp, peeled

Yield: 3 servings

Sauté onion and green pepper in olive oil in skillet. Add tomato sauce, Ro-Tel tomatoes, garlic and pepper to taste. Simmer until heated through. Add shrimp. Simmer until shrimp are tender. Serve over hot cooked rice.

Approx Per Serving: Cal 300; Prot 34.6 g; Carbo 15.8 g; T Fat 11.3 g; Chol 295.0 mg; Potas 922.0 mg; Sod 952.0 mg.

Steve Robinson, Kentucky

SHRIMP CREOLE

1 8-ounce can tomato sauce
1 4-ounce can sliced
mushrooms, drained
¹/2 cup dry white wine
¹/2 cup chopped onion
1 clove of garlic, minced
¹/2 cup chopped green bell
pepper
¹/2 cup chopped celery
2 bay leaves
¹/2 teaspoon red pepper flakes
1 pound shrimp, peeled
2 cups hot cooked rice

Yield: 4 servings

Combine tomato sauce, mushrooms, wine, onion, garlic, green pepper, celery, bay leaves and red pepper in skillet; mix well. Bring to a boil; reduce heat. Simmer, covered, for 10 minutes. Add shrimp; mix well. Uncover. Cook for 3 to 4 minutes or until shrimp are pink. Serve over rice. Discard bay leaves.

Approx Per Serving: Cal 289; Prot 26.9 g; Carbo 34.6 g; T Fat 2.4 g; Chol 172.0 mg; Potas 609.0 mg; Sod 661.8 mg.

Richard McCoy, Oklahoma

SEAFOOD CASSEROLE

2 6½-ounce cans crab meat,
     drained
1 4-ounce can shrimp, drained
1 10-ounce package frozen
     peas, thawed
1½ cups cooked rice
¼ cup chopped green bell
     pepper
2 tablespoons chopped parsley
1 cup sour cream

Yield: 6 servings

Combine crab meat, shrimp, peas, rice, green pepper, parsley and sour cream in bowl; toss to mix. Pour into 2-quart casserole sprayed with nonstick cooking spray. Bake, covered, at 350 degrees for 1 hour.

Approx Per Serving: Cal 262; Prot 22.3 g; Carbo 21.0 g; T Fat 9.5 g; Chol 108.0 mg; Potas 429.0 mg; Sod 315.3 mg.

Carrol Pauley, Montana

SEAFOOD MEDLEY

1 pound shrimp, peeled
¼ cup margarine
1 pound scallops
1 pound crab meat, drained,
     flaked
½ cup bread crumbs
Worcestershire sauce to taste
1 clove of garlic, crushed
Juice of 1 lemon

Yield: 6 servings

Sauté shrimp in margarine in skillet for 5 minutes; stirring frequently. Add scallops. Sauté for 5 minutes; stirring frequently. Add crab meat. Heat for 5 minutes. Spoon into ramekins. Sprinkle bread crumbs, Worcestershire sauce, garlic and lemon juice over seafood. Bake at 350 degrees for 15 minutes or until golden brown.

Approx Per Serving: Cal 322; Prot 45.0 g; Carbo 8.7 g; T Fat 10.8 g; Chol 248.3 mg; Potas 652.0 mg; Sod 628.0 mg.

Amy Mills, Maryland

POACHED SALMON

8 6-ounce fresh or frozen
     salmon steaks
½ cup white wine
1 cup water
2 tablespoons wine vinegar
½ cup chopped celery leaves
¼ bay leaf
7 peppercorns
1 teaspoon dillweed
5 whole allspice

Yield: 8 servings

Wash salmon and pat dry. Combine wine, water, vinegar and seasonings in skillet. Add salmon. Simmer, tightly covered, over medium heat for 8 to 10 minutes or until fish flakes easily. Drain well. Serve on heated platter garnished with watercress or parsley.

Approx Per Serving: Cal 255; Prot 33.8 g; Carbo 1.2 g; T Fat 10.9 g; Chol 93.6 mg; Potas 860.0 mg; Sod 77.0 mg.

Butler McGee, Hawaii

FILLETS OF SOLE BONNE FEMME

2 shallots, chopped
2 tablespoons margarine
2¹/₂ pounds sole fillets
8 mushrooms, sliced
¹/₈ teaspoon pepper
1 cup dry white wine
1 tablespoon chopped parsley
2 tablespoons margarine
1¹/₂ tablespoons flour

Yield: 6 servings

Sauté shallots in 2 tablespoons margarine in large skillet for 2 minutes. Wash fillets and pat dry. Arrange over shallots. Top with mushrooms. Sprinkle with pepper. Add wine. Bring to a boil; reduce heat. Simmer, covered, for 10 minutes. Add parsley. Cook for 5 minutes longer or until fish flakes easily. Drain well, reserving 1 cup cooking liquid. Place fish and mushrooms in 8x12-inch baking dish. Melt 2 tablespoons margarine in skillet. Stir in flour. Add reserved liquid gradually. Cook over medium heat until thickened, stirring constantly. Pour over fish. Broil for 3 to 5 minutes or until top is golden brown.

Approx Per Serving: Cal 328; Prot 37.9 g; Carbo 14.7 g; T Fat 10.0 g; Chol 90.0 mg; Potas 985.0 mg; Sod 227.0 mg.

Ruthann Bird, Texas

TUNA DELIGHT

¹/₂ onion, chopped
3 tablespoons oil
2 cups cooked rice
1 16-ounce can French-style green beans
1 6¹/₂-ounce can flaked tuna, drained
1 can cream of mushroom soup

Yield: 8 servings

Sauté onion in oil in skillet until tender. Add rice and green beans; mix well. Stir in tuna and mushroom soup. Cook until heated through.

Approx Per Serving: Cal 200; Prot 9.1 g; Carbo 18.5 g; T Fat 10.0 g; Chol 4.5 mg; Potas 165.0 mg; Sod 533.0 mg.

Margaret Parks, Connecticut

MICROWAVE TUNA AND RICE CASSEROLE

3 ounces cream cheese, softened
1 can cream of mushroom soup
1 6-ounce can tuna, drained
2 cups cooked rice
¹/₄ cup chopped green onions
1 tablespoon chopped parsley
¹/₈ teaspoon pepper
¹/₄ cup Parmesan cheese
Paprika to taste

Yield: 6 servings

Blend cream cheese and soup in bowl. Add tuna, rice, green onions, parsley and pepper; mix well. Spoon into 1¹/₂-quart glass baking dish. Top with cheese and paprika. Microwave on High for 4 to 6 minutes or until heated through.

Approx Per Serving: Cal 207; Prot 12.5 g; Carbo 21.0 g; T Fat 7.8 g; Chol 25.4 mg; Potas 178.0 mg; Sod 554.0 mg.

Martha Stacey, Oklahoma

ARTICHOKE FRITTATA

2   6-ounce jars marinated
      artichokes
1 onion, chopped
4 eggs, beaten
1/4 cup dry bread crumbs
1/8 teaspoon garlic salt
1/8 teaspoon pepper
1/8 teaspoon oregano
2 cups grated Cheddar cheese
1/2 cup Parmesan cheese
2 tablespoons minced parsley

Yield: 12 servings

Drain artichokes, reserving marinade from 1 jar. Place reserved marinade in skillet; add onion. Sauté until onion is tender. Combine eggs, bread crumbs, garlic salt, pepper and oregano in bowl; mix well. Add cheeses, parsley and artichokes; mix well. Add to onion mixture; mix well. Pour into 9x13-inch baking pan sprayed with nonstick cooking spray. Bake at 325 degrees for 30 minutes. Cool. Cut into squares.

Approx Per Serving: Cal 159; Prot 9.3 g; Carbo 5.3 g; T Fat 11.5 g; Chol 114.0 mg; Potas 144.0 mg; Sod 391.0 mg.

Ransom Denton, Mississippi

EGGS À LA GOLDENROD

6 hard-boiled eggs
3 tablespoons margarine
1/2 teaspoon dry mustard
1/4 teaspoon pepper
Dash of nutmeg
1/2 teaspoon basil
2 teaspoons instant chicken
      bouillon
2 tablespoons cornstarch
2 cups milk
1 teaspoon tarragon vinegar
6 slices bread, toasted

Yield: 6 servings

Cut eggs into halves, removing yolks. Press yolks through sieve. Chop egg whites. Melt margarine in saucepan. Stir in dry mustard, pepper, nutmeg, basil, bouillon and cornstarch. Add milk gradually. Cook until thickened, stirring constantly. Add vinegar and egg whites; mix well. Arrange toast on warm serving dish. Spoon sauce over toast. Top with sieved egg yolks. Garnish with paprika.

Approx Per Serving: Cal 271; Prot 11.4 g; Carbo 21.3 g; T Fat 15.2 g; Chol 285.0 mg; Potas 271.0 mg; Sod 677.0 mg.

Suzanne Scarborough, Ohio

BAKED OMELET

12 eggs
3/4 cup cottage cheese
1 cup chopped green onions
1 cup chopped green bell pepper
1 1/2 cups fresh bean sprouts
1 cup sliced fresh mushrooms
1/2 cup chopped cashews
2 tomatoes, sliced
1 cup shredded Cheddar cheese

Yield: 12 servings

Beat eggs and cottage cheese in mixer bowl. Add onions and next 4 ingredients; mix well. Pour into greased 9x13-inch casserole. Arrange tomatoes over top. Sprinkle with cheese. Bake at 350 degrees for 45 minutes. Cut into squares.

Approx Per Serving: Cal 177; Prot 11.9 g; Carbo 5.5 g; T Fat 12.0 g; Chol 286.0 mg; Potas 236.0 mg; Sod 221.5 mg.

Shirley Whaley, Arizona

Vegetable Chili

1/4 cup chopped onion
1 clove of garlic, minced
2 tablespoons oil
2 16-ounce cans whole
    tomatoes
3 cups sliced mushrooms
2 cups chopped green bell
    peppers
2 cups sliced zucchini
1 tablespoon chili powder
1 teaspoon oregano
1/2 teaspoon cumin
1/8 teaspoon pepper
1 1/2 tablespoons flour
3 tablespoons cold water
1 8-ounce can kidney beans,
    drained
1/2 cup shredded Cheddar
    cheese

Yield: 8 servings

Sauté onion and garlic in hot oil in large skillet until onion is tender. Add tomatoes, mushrooms, green peppers, zucchini, chili powder, oregano, cumin and pepper. Cook over low heat for 15 minutes, stirring frequently. Blend flour with water. Add to chili. Stir in beans. Heat to serving temperature, stirring occasionally. Garnish with Cheddar cheese.

Approx Per Serving: Cal 135; Prot 6.0 g; Carbo 15.3 g; T Fat 6.6 g; Chol 7.1 mg; Potas 291.0 mg; Sod 348.0 mg.

Lena Allison, West Virginia

Red and Yellow Bell Pepper Pasta

6 cups thinly sliced onions
2 large red bell peppers, cut
    into thin strips
2 large yellow bell peppers, cut
    into thin strips
3 tablespoons sugar
3 tablespoons olive oil
2 cups chicken broth
1/4 cup cornstarch
1/4 cup water
1 tablespoon grated lemon rind
2 tablespoons lemon juice
1 teaspoon basil
1 teaspoon mint
1/2 teaspoon salt
12 ounces tomato and spinach
    twist pasta, cooked
2 tablespoons Parmesan cheese

Yield: 6 servings

Sauté onions, peppers and sugar in olive oil for 2 to 3 minutes until softened; set aside. Combine broth, cornstarch dissolved in water, lemon rind, lemon juice, basil, mint and salt in medium saucepan; mix well. Cook over medium heat, stirring constantly. Add sautéed vegetables. Heat to serving temperature. Serve over hot pasta. Sprinkle with Parmesan cheese.

Approx Per Serving: Cal 393; Prot 12.0 g; Carbo 67.0 g; T Fat 10.0 g; Chol 1.9 mg; Sod 305.0 mg.

Photograph for this recipe is on the cover.

Light Spaghetti Primavera

1 8-ounce package spaghetti
½ cup low-calorie Italian
  dressing
1 green bell pepper, chopped
1 red bell pepper, chopped
1 yellow squash, cut into
  julienne strips
1 cup sliced fresh mushrooms
¼ cup chopped onion
3 tablespoons sliced black
  olives
¼ cup shredded mozzarella
  cheese
3 tablespoons chopped fresh
  parsley

Yield: 6 servings

Cook spaghetti using package directions; drain. Combine dressing, bell peppers, squash, mushrooms, onion and olives in skillet. Stir-fry until tender-crisp. Serve immediately over hot spaghetti. Sprinkle with cheese and parsley.

Approx Per Serving: Cal 194; Prot 6.6 g; Carbo 33.6 g; T Fat 4.1 g; Chol 4.8 mg; Potas 262.0 mg; Sod 233.0 mg.

Michelle Shelton, Texas

Vegetable Pasta

⅓ cup thinly sliced celery
⅓ cup green beans, cut into
  ½-inch pieces
⅓ cup finely chopped carrots
⅓ cup sliced red onion
2 tablespoons chopped green
  bell pepper
½ teaspoon basil
⅛ teaspoon garlic powder
¼ teaspoon salt
  Pepper to taste
1 teaspoon oil
⅓ cup frozen green peas
1 teaspoon margarine
2 tablespoons flour
¾ cup skim milk
2 quarts boiling water
1 teaspoon salt
4 ounces thin spaghetti

Yield: 4 servings

Sauté celery, green beans, carrots, onion, green pepper, basil, garlic powder, ¼ teaspoon salt and pepper in oil in skillet for 5 minutes, stirring constantly. Stir in frozen peas. Reduce heat. Cook, covered, for 2 minutes or until vegetables are tender-crisp. Remove vegetables to heat-proof bowl; keep warm. Melt margarine in skillet. Stir in flour. Add milk gradually, stirring constantly. Cook until thickened. Combine water and 1 teaspoon salt in saucepan. Bring to a boil. Drop spaghetti into boiling water; reduce heat. Cook for 9 to 11 minutes; drain. Place in large bowl. Toss with white sauce. Stir in vegetables; mix gently.

Approx Per Serving: Cal 178; Prot 6.7 g; Carbo 31.5 g; T Fat 2.7 g; Chol 0.8 mg; Potas 278.0 mg; Sod 193.0 mg.

Kris Justin, Pennsylvania

Vegetables
& Side Dishes

VEGETABLES & SIDE DISHES

What is it about the sight of a pristine, raw vegetable that makes us want to whip up something saucy? Where did we ever get the idea that a plain, unvarnished, ungarnished garden goody was inelegant, a pitiful thing that needs to be augmented with cheese, brown sugar, parsley, crumbs or even, shudder, marshmallows?

Back in the days when vegetables and fruits were hard to come by unless you had your own garden to rely on, there may have been some justification for all this dolling up. And in times when canned varieties were all that was available, hiding them in cream sauce may have been the kindest way to serve them.

Today, our tastes have moved toward the lighter side, and we've come to appreciate the natural good taste. That's not to say, though, that a cheesy broccoli casserole doesn't have its place on the list of life's delights or that those special holiday side dishes are a thing of the past. We've just come up with a bushel basket full of ways to make them part of your healthy-eating lifestyle.

When it comes to vegetables and side dishes, substitution is the name of the game. When a recipe calls for butter, use margarine or diet margarine (but don't try to fry or bake with diet margarine, as it has too much water). Frequently you may substitute up to half of the fat called for in a recipe with bouillon, fruit juice or other liquid. Remember, though, that fat does not evaporate like these other liquids, and use slightly more of them, accordingly.

Some vegetable dishes call for canned cream soups, which are high in fat (16 grams per can) or mayonnaise (a killer at 180 grams of fat per cup). Instead of a can of soup, try one 12-ounce can of evaporated skim milk, 1 teaspoon chicken bouillon and 2 tablespoons of flour to thicken. Replace a cup of mayonnaise with ¼ cup low-fat mayonnaise and 1 cup low-fat plain yogurt.

In general, you can use less cheese than called for in a recipe. The more flavorful the cheese the better, so try using half as much Cheddar as is called for, but use extra sharp Cheddar for the same tasty effect.

Remember that appearance is often half the battle when you're trying to feed vegetables to your family. Try shredding carrots into a colorful haystack before briefly steaming them. Or simmer zucchini in tomato juice with a little onion, garlic, basil and oregano until tender, then broil with a little Parmesan sprinkled on top.

Cooking light really comes into its own where vegetables are concerned, and this chapter's bumper crop of recipes lets their natural goodness and fresh flavor shine.

Green Beans Parmesan

2 10-ounce packages frozen
French-style green beans
3/4 cup (about) milk
1/4 cup chopped onion
2 tablespoons margarine
2 tablespoons flour
2 tablespoons Parmesan cheese
1 5-ounce can sliced water
chestnuts, drained
3/4 cup soft bread crumbs
2 tablespoons Parmesan cheese
2 tablespoons melted margarine

Yield: 8 servings

Cook beans using package directions. Drain, reserving liquid. Add enough milk to reserved liquid to measure 1 1/4 cups; set aside. Sauté onion in 2 tablespoons margarine in saucepan. Stir in flour. Stir in milk mixture all at once. Cook until thickened, stirring constantly. Stir in 2 tablespoons cheese. Add beans and water chestnuts; mix well. Spoon into 1-quart baking dish. Toss crumbs and 2 tablespoons cheese with 2 tablespoons melted margarine in small bowl. Sprinkle over casserole. Bake at 350 degrees for 30 minutes or until bubbly.

Approx Per Serving: Cal 124; Prot 3.6 g;
Carbo 11.6 g; T Fat 7.6 g; Chol 4.6 mg;
Potas 150.0 mg; Sod 148.0 mg.

Barbara Papineau, Georgia

Mushrooms and Green Beans

1 20-ounce can green beans
1 4-ounce can sliced
mushrooms, drained
1 8-ounce jar small whole
onions, drained
1 tablespoon margarine

Yield: 4 servings

Simmer undrained beans in saucepan until heated through; drain. Add remaining ingredients. Simmer for 5 minutes.

Approx Per Serving: Cal 79; Prot 2.9 g;
Carbo 12.0 g; T Fat 3.2 g; Chol 0.0 mg;
Potas 280.0 mg; Sod 511.0 mg.

Helen Kinsella, Oregon

Cajun Green Beans

1 medium onion
1/2 green bell pepper
1/2 pound mushrooms
2 tablespoons margarine
2 16-ounce cans French-style
green beans, drained
1 can mushroom soup
1 6-ounce roll garlic cheese,
shredded
1/2 teaspoon garlic powder
1/4 teaspoon white pepper

Yield: 12 servings

Chop onion and green pepper; slice mushrooms. Sauté onion, green pepper and mushrooms in margarine in large skillet until glazed. Add beans, soup and cheese. Simmer until cheese is melted, stirring frequently. Add garlic powder, white pepper and black pepper to taste; mix well. Spoon into 2-quart casserole. Bake at 350 degrees for 45 minutes to 1 hour.

Approx Per Serving: Cal 115; Prot 4.5 g;
Carbo 8.6 g; T Fat 7.5 g; Chol 9.5 mg;
Potas 252.0 mg; Sod 545.0 mg.

Rebecca Gallatin, Ohio

Broccoli and Onion Deluxe

2 10-ounce packages frozen
cut broccoli
2 cups frozen whole small
onions
2 tablespoons margarine
2 tablespoons flour
Dash of pepper
1 cup milk
3 ounces cream cheese
2 tablespoons margarine
1 cup soft bread crumbs
1/4 cup Parmesan cheese

Yield: 10 servings

Cook broccoli and onions in separate saucepans using package directions for each; drain. Melt 2 tablespoons margarine in saucepan. Stir in flour and pepper. Add milk. Cook until thickened, stirring constantly. Reduce heat to low. Add cream cheese. Cook until cream cheese melts, stirring constantly. Add vegetables. Pour into 1 1/2-quart casserole. Bake at 350 degrees for 20 minutes. Melt remaining 2 tablespoons margarine in saucepan. Stir in bread crumbs and Parmesan cheese. Sprinkle over casserole. Bake until crumbs are brown.

Approx Per Serving: Cal 141; Prot 4.9 g; Carbo 10.9 g; T Fat 9.3 g; Chol 14.6 mg; Potas 201.0 mg; Sod 147.7 mg.

Margie Albee, Connecticut

Renaissance Red Cabbage

1 5-pound head red cabbage,
shredded
1 cup dry white Burgundy
3 tablespoons white vinegar
1/4 teaspoon salt
1/8 teaspoon pepper
1/8 teaspoon cloves
2 teaspoons cinnamon
2 whole bay leaves
2 tablespoons sugar
1/4 cup cranberry sauce
2 apples, peeled, cut into
1/2-inch cubes
1/2 cup sweetened applesauce

Yield: 16 servings

Combine cabbage, wine and vinegar in large saucepan; cover. Bring to a boil; reduce heat. Cook, covered, over low heat for 5 minutes. Add salt, pepper, cloves, cinnamon, bay leaves, sugar, cranberry sauce and apples; mix well. Cook for 20 minutes longer. Stir in applesauce. Discard bay leaves.

Approx Per Serving: Cal 77; Prot 2.0 g; Carbo 16.4 g; T Fat 0.4 g; Chol 0.0 mg; Potas 329.0 mg; Sod 51.8 mg.

Rosalinda Pruitt, Alabama

CABBAGE DELUXE

1/4 cup oil
1 small head cabbage, chopped
1 cup chopped celery
1/2 cup chopped onion
1 cup chopped tomatoes

Yield: 8 servings

Coat bottom of skillet with oil. Layer cabbage, celery, onion and tomatoes in prepared skillet. Sprinkle with salt and pepper to taste. Cook, covered, over medium heat for 30 minutes or until vegetables are tender.

Approx Per Serving: Cal 78; Prot 0.8 g; Carbo 4.1 g; T Fat 7.0 g; Chol 0.0 mg; Potas 191.0 mg; Sod 21.3 mg.

Edna Clinton, Pennsylvania

COPPER KETTLE CARROTS

2 cups shredded carrots
2 cups finely sliced green onions
1/4 cup margarine
1/4 cup chicken broth
3/4 teaspoon fennel
3 tablespoons Grand Marnier

Yield: 6 servings

Stir-fry carrots and onions in margarine in large skillet until onions are clear. Add chicken broth; mix well. Simmer, covered, just until carrots are tender. Add fennel. Stir in Grand Marnier just before serving. Garnish with chopped parsley. May substitute nutmeg or anise for fennel and Triple Sec or Cointreau for Grand Marnier.

Approx Per Serving: Cal 125; Prot 1.2 g; Carbo 9.1 g; T Fat 7.9 g; Chol 0.0 mg; Potas 215.0 mg; Sod 111.0 mg.

Lisa Jo Parkinson, Utah

CRUNCHY SURPRISE CARROTS AND PEAS

1 cup thinly sliced carrots
1 cup water
20 ounces frozen peas
1/4 cup maple syrup
1 8-ounce can sliced mushrooms, drained
1 8-ounce can sliced water chestnuts, drained
1/4 cup cornstarch

Yield: 10 servings

Combine carrots and water in heavy 3-quart saucepan. Simmer, covered, for 5 minutes. Add peas. Simmer, covered, for 3 minutes. Add maple syrup, mushrooms and water chestnuts; mix well. Bring to a boil. Remove vegetables with slotted spoon to serving dish. Stir cornstarch into remaining liquid. Cook for 1 minute or until thickened, stirring constantly. Pour over warm vegetables.

Approx Per Serving: Cal 98; Prot 3.7 g; Carbo 21.2 g; T Fat 0.3 g; Chol 0.0 mg; Potas 186.0 mg; Sod 174.0 mg.

Jill Brown, Indiana

Orange-Glazed Carrots

1½ tablespoons margarine
⅓ cup packed brown sugar
⅓ cup frozen orange juice
concentrate
6 cups cooked sliced carrots

Yield: 8 servings

Melt margarine in skillet. Blend in brown sugar and orange juice concentrate. Stir in carrots. Cook over medium-high heat for 1 minute or until heated through, stirring frequently.

Approx Per Serving: Cal 124; Prot 1.6 g; Carbo 25.5 g; T Fat 2.4 g; Chol 0.0 mg; Potas 376.0 mg; Sod 100.0 mg.

Lillian Sublette, Montana

Cauliflower with Peanut Crumb Topping

1 head cauliflower
2 tablespoons finely chopped
salted peanuts
¾ cup dry bread crumbs
2 tablespoons peanut oil

Yield: 6 servings

Cook cauliflower in salted water to cover in saucepan for 15 to 20 minutes or until tender; drain. Combine peanuts, bread crumbs and oil in bowl; mix well. Place cauliflower in serving dish. Sprinkle with topping.

Approx Per Serving: Cal 90; Prot 2.7 g; Carbo 6.9 g; T Fat 6.3 g; Chol 0.2 mg; Potas 265.0 mg; Sod 53.0 mg.

Millie Minor, Arizona

Baked Corn

2 tablespoons low-fat
margarine
1   20-ounce can cream-style
corn
¼ cup skim milk
1 tablespoon sugar
½ teaspoon low-sodium salt
1 tablespoon flour
½ cup egg substitute
¼ cup chopped green bell
pepper

Yield: 5 servings

Melt margarine in 1½-quart casserole sprayed with nonstick cooking spray. Combine corn, milk, sugar, salt, flour, egg substitute and green pepper in large bowl; mix well. Spoon into casserole. Bake at 350 degrees for 30 minutes.

Approx Per Serving: Cal 144; Prot 5.6 g; Carbo 25.3 g; T Fat 3.6 g; Chol 0.5 mg; Potas 418.0 mg; Sod 539.0 mg.

Mark Connelly, Idaho

CORN PUDDING

1 tablespoon melted margarine
1 cup milk
2 eggs, beaten
1/4 cup sugar
1 cup corn

Yield: 6 servings

Pour margarine into casserole. Combine milk, eggs, sugar and corn in bowl; mix well. Pour into prepared 1-quart casserole. Bake at 350 degrees for 1 hour.

Approx Per Serving: Cal 122; Prot 4.2 g; Carbo 15.3 g; T Fat 5.4 g; Chol 97.0 mg; Potas 146.0 mg; Sod 60.2 mg.

Jean Austin, West Virginia

EGGPLANT CASSEROLE

1 eggplant, chopped
1 onion, chopped
1　8-ounce can tomato sauce
1/2 cup cottage cheese
2 medium tomatoes, chopped
1 teaspoon marjoram
1/2 teaspoon pepper

Yield: 8 servings

Sauté eggplant and onion in large skillet until tender. Stir in tomato sauce, cottage cheese, tomatoes, marjoram and pepper. Spoon into greased 9x13-inch baking dish. Bake at 325 degrees for 35 minutes.

Approx Per Serving: Cal 40; Prot 2.8 g; Carbo 6.5 g; T Fat 0.7 g; Chol 1.9 mg; Potas 256.0 mg; Sod 228.0 mg.

Lola Givens, Minnesota

STUFFED EGGPLANT

1 medium eggplant
1 medium onion, chopped
1/4 cup chopped parsley
1 tablespoon margarine
1 can cream of mushroom soup
1/8 teaspoon Worcestershire sauce
1 cup crushed butter crackers

Yield: 6 servings

Cut a lengthwise slice from side of eggplant. Scoop out pulp, leaving 1/4 to 1/2-inch thick shell. Cook eggplant pulp in water to cover in saucepan until tender, stirring occasionally; drain. Sauté onion and parsley in margarine in skillet until onion is tender. Combine cooked eggplant, onion, parsley and soup in bowl; mix well. Add Worcestershire sauce and pepper to taste; mix well. Reserve 1 tablespoon cracker crumbs. Add enough remaining cracker crumbs to make a thick but moist mixture. Spoon into eggplant shell. Sprinkle reserved cracker crumbs over top. Place in 1 1/2-quart casserole. Place casserole in baking pan half filled with water. Bake at 325 degrees for 25 to 30 minutes or until brown.

Approx Per Serving: Cal 130; Prot 2.2 g; Carbo 14.2 g; T Fat 8.4 g; Chol 0.6 mg; Potas 191.0 mg; Sod 518.0 mg.

Alice Armstrong, New Jersey

OKRA OLÉ

4 cups sliced okra
1 cup chopped onion
2 tomatoes, coarsely chopped
2 jalapeño peppers, chopped
1/4 cup oil

Yield: 12 servings

Place okra, onion, tomatoes, peppers and salt and pepper to taste in hot oil in skillet. Cook over medium heat for 25 to 30 minutes or until tender, stirring frequently.

Approx Per Serving: Cal 73; Prot 1.7 g; Carbo 7.2 g; T Fat 4.8 g; Chol 0.0 mg; Potas 214.0 mg; Sod 86.8 mg.

Clinton Miller, Mississippi

ONIONS PARMESAN

8 medium onions, sliced
1/4 cup margarine
1/2 cup Parmesan cheese

Yield: 6 servings

Sauté onions in margarine in skillet for 10 to 12 minutes. Place in 2 1/2-quart baking dish. Sprinkle with cheese. Broil 5 inches from heat source until cheese melts.

Approx Per Serving: Cal 170; Prot 5.4 g; Carbo 15.9 g; T Fat 10.2 g; Chol 4.3 mg; Potas 340.0 mg; Sod 194.0 mg.

Ellen Wrigley, New Mexico

BEST PARSNIPS

1 pound parsnips, peeled
1 tablespoon margarine
1 teaspoon dry mustard
1/3 cup packed brown sugar

Yield: 4 servings

Cut parsnips into 2-inch strips. Combine with water to cover in saucepan. Simmer for 20 minutes or just until tender, stirring occasionally; drain. Add margarine, mustard and brown sugar; mix well. Pour into serving dish. May double recipe, cook for several minutes longer and mash.

Approx Per Serving: Cal 178; Prot 1.4 g; Carbo 37.9 g; T Fat 3.2 g; Chol 0.0 mg; Potas 489.0 mg; Sod 44.0 mg.

Jo Ann Carpenter, Texas

Oven-Fried Potatoes

8 large baking potatoes
1/2 cup oil
2 tablespoons Parmesan cheese
1/2 teaspoon garlic powder
1/2 teaspoon paprika
1/4 teaspoon pepper

Yield: 16 servings

Cut each potato into 8 wedges. Place peel side down in shallow baking dish. Brush wedges with mixture of oil, cheese, garlic powder, paprika and pepper. Bake at 375 degrees for 45 minutes or until potatoes are tender and golden brown, brushing occasionally with oil mixture.

Approx Per Serving: Cal 173; Prot 2.6 g; Carbo 25.6 g; T Fat 7.1 g; Chol 0.5 mg; Potas 424.0 mg; Sod 20.0 mg.

Constance Sales, Kentucky

Rutabaga Casserole

1 large rutabaga, peeled, cut into cubes
1/8 teaspoon salt
3 eggs, beaten
2 cups milk
3 tablespoons flour
1/2 teaspoon salt
1/8 teaspoon pepper

Yield: 8 servings

Cook rutabaga with 1/8 teaspoon salt in water to cover in saucepan until tender; drain. Mash rutabaga but leave lumpy. Place in 2-quart casserole. Combine eggs, milk, flour, salt and pepper in bowl; mix well. Pour over rutabaga. Bake for 2 hours or until casserole is set and resembles custard.

Approx Per Serving: Cal 97; Prot 5.2 g; Carbo 9.6 g; T Fat 4.3 g; Chol 111.0 mg; Potas 286.0 mg; Sod 230.0 mg.

Elinor Donahue, South Dakota

Grilled Tomatoes

8 firm ripe tomatoes
Oregano to taste
1/2 cup shredded Cheddar cheese
1/4 cup margarine

Yield: 8 servings

Cut each tomato in half; sprinkle with salt, pepper and oregano to taste. Place each on square of heavy-duty foil. Sprinkle with cheese; dot with margarine. Fold foil securely around tomato half. Cook on grill over moderate heat for 10 to 15 minutes.

Approx Per Serving: Cal 103; Prot 2.9 g; Carbo 5.4 g; T Fat 8.4 g; Chol 23.0 mg; Potas 264.0 mg; Sod 86.5 mg.

Sue Hudson, Tennessee

Italian Zucchini Casserole

4 cups thinly sliced zucchini
1 cup chopped onion
1/2 cup margarine
1/2 cup chopped fresh parsley
1/2 teaspoon pepper
1/4 teaspoon basil
1/4 teaspoon oregano
2 eggs, well beaten
2 cups shredded mozzarella cheese
1 8-count package crescent rolls
2 teaspoons prepared mustard

Yield: 8 servings

Sauté zucchini and onion in margarine in skillet for 10 minutes or until tender. Add parsley, pepper, basil and oregano; mix well. Mix eggs and cheese in bowl. Stir in zucchini mixture. Line 10-inch pie plate with crescent roll dough, pressing edges to seal perforations. Spread with mustard. Spoon zucchini mixture into crust. Bake at 375 degrees for 18 to 20 minutes or until knife inserted in center comes out clean. Cover edges of crust with foil for last 10 minutes of baking to prevent overbrowning.

Approx Per Serving: Cal 302; Prot 8.5 g; Carbo 12.4 g; T Fat 21.0 g; Chol 81.0 mg; Potas 306.0 mg; Sod 514.8 mg.

Ann Bowman, Virginia

Marinated Fresh Vegetables

1/2 cup white wine vinegar
1 cup water
1 tablespoon olive oil
1 clove of garlic, thinly sliced
1/2 teaspoon paprika
1/4 teaspoon pepper
2 medium carrots, cut into matchstick pieces
1 stalk celery, cut into matchstick pieces
1 medium zucchini, cut into matchstick pieces
1 small red bell pepper, cut into matchstick pieces
1 tablespoon drained capers

Yield: 4 servings

Combine vinegar, water, olive oil, garlic, paprika and pepper in bowl; mix well. Add carrots, celery, zucchini, red pepper and capers; toss well. Chill, covered, overnight.

Approx Per Serving: Cal 64; Prot 1.1 g; Carbo 8.6 g; T Fat 3.7 g; Chol 0.0 mg; Potas 318.0 mg; Sod 23.6 mg.

Donna Bates, Ohio

STIR-FRY VEGETABLES

4 cups shredded cabbage
1 green bell pepper, thinly sliced
2 large onions, thinly sliced
2 large tomatoes, cut into wedges
3 tablespoons oil
2 teaspoons sugar
1/4 teaspoon pepper

Yield: 6 servings

Combine vegetables in bowl; toss to mix. Add to hot oil in large skillet; sprinkle with sugar and pepper. Cook, covered, over medium heat for 10 minutes, stirring twice.

Approx Per Serving: Cal 106; Prot 1.7 g; Carbo 10.5 g; T Fat 7.2 g; Chol 0.0 mg; Potas 315.0 mg; Sod 13.5 mg.

Sue Coates, Wisconsin

GREEN AND GOLD PILAF

1 1/2 cups uncooked long grain rice
3 tablespoons margarine
3 cups water
6 chicken bouillon cubes
1/4 teaspoon white pepper
3 small carrots
1   10-ounce package frozen French-style green beans

Yield: 8 servings

Combine rice, margarine, water, bouillon cubes and pepper in saucepan. Bring to a boil; reduce heat. Simmer, covered, for 15 minutes or until rice is tender. Cut carrots into short thin sticks. Add carrots and thawed beans to rice. Let stand, covered, for 5 minutes. Season to taste.

Approx Per Serving: Cal 188; Prot 3.6 g; Carbo 32.8 g; T Fat 4.7 g; Chol 0.0 mg; Potas 273.0 mg; Sod 913.0 mg.

Dorothy Chapman, Kansas

LOW-CALORIE CRANBERRY SAUCE

1 cup whole cranberries
1 cup water
2 tablespoons sugar
1 small package sugar-free cherry gelatin
3/4 cup water
2 packets sugar substitute

Yield: 4 servings

Grind cranberries in food processor container. Combine with 1 cup water and sugar in saucepan. Bring mixture to a hard boil, stirring constantly; remove from heat. Dissolve gelatin in hot cranberry mixture. Stir in remaining 3/4 cup water and sugar substitute. Pour into bowls. Chill until set.

Approx Per Serving: Cal 40; Prot 0.8 g; Carbo 9.2 g; T Fat 0.0 g; Chol 0.0 mg; Potas 17.0 mg; Sod 50.0 mg.

Wanda Lawrence, New York

HOT MUSTARD SAUCE

3 tablespoons dry mustard
1/4 cup water
1/4 cup vinegar
2 tablespoons sugar
1/8 teaspoon salt
1 egg, slightly beaten
1/2 cup mayonnaise

Yield: 16 tablespoons

Combine dry mustard, water and vinegar in bowl; mix well. Let stand overnight. Add sugar, salt and egg; mix well. Pour into double boiler. Cook until mixture thickens. Chill in refrigerator. Add mayonnaise just before serving; mix well.

Approx Per Tablespoon: Cal 61; Prot 0.5 g; Carbo 2.0 g; T Fat 5.8 g; Chol 21.2 mg; Potas 10.3 mg; Sod 60.8 mg.

Janice Lindsey, Vermont

TOMATO SAUCE

1/4 cup oil
3 medium onions, thinly sliced
3 large carrots, thinly sliced
2 medium green bell peppers, finely chopped
1 clove of garlic, minced
1   12-ounce can tomato paste
12 large tomatoes, peeled, finely chopped
1/4 cup packed brown sugar
2 teaspoons oregano
1 1/4 teaspoons basil
1/2 teaspoon pepper

Yield: 16 cups

Heat oil in heavy saucepan. Add onions, carrots, green peppers and garlic. Cook until vegetables are tender, stirring occasionally. Add tomato paste, tomatoes, brown sugar and seasonings. Bring to a boil. Boil for 2 minutes. Simmer, partially covered, for 2 hours, stirring occasionally. May be canned or frozen. For freezer storage, spoon cold sauce into freezer bags; seal tightly.

Approx Per Cup: Cal 99; Prot 2.3 g; Carbo 15.8 g; T Fat 4.0 g; Chol 0.0 mg; Potas 525.0 mg; Sod 29.0 mg.

Connie Walker, South Carolina

SWEET AND SOUR SAUCE

1/2 cup sugar
1/2 cup vinegar
2 tablespoons soy sauce
3 tablespoons tomato sauce
1   8-ounce can pineapple chunks
2 tablespoons cornstarch

Yield: 35 tablespoons

Combine sugar, vinegar, soy sauce and tomato sauce in saucepan. Bring to a boil. Drain pineapple, reserving juice. Stir pineapple into hot sauce. Dissolve cornstarch in reserved juice. Add to sauce. Simmer until thickened, stirring constantly. May substitute catsup for tomato sauce.

Approx Per Tablespoon: Cal 19; Prot 0.1 g; Carbo 4.9 g; T Fat 0.0 g; Chol 0.0 mg; Potas 17.0 mg; Sod 66.9 mg.

Minnie Wilson, Louisiana

HOMEMADE BARBECUE SAUCE

1 cup catsup
1/4 cup packed brown sugar
1/3 cup cider vinegar
1/2 teaspoon dillweed
1/2 teaspoon garlic powder

Yield: 28 tablespoons

Combine catsup, brown sugar and vinegar in saucepan. Bring to a boil. Remove from heat. Add dillweed and garlic powder; mix well. The ingredients in this easy, make-ahead recipe can be varied to taste.

Approx Per Tablespoon: Cal 18; Prot 0.2 g; Carbo 4.6 g; T Fat 0.0 g; Chol 0.0 mg; Potas 46.2 mg; Sod 103.0 mg.

Maureen Benson, Idaho

BASIC WHITE SAUCE MIX

1/2 cup flour
1 cup nonfat dry milk powder

Yield: 24 tablespoons

Combine flour and milk powder in 1-pint jar; cover with lid. Shake to mix well. May store in refrigerator for 4 weeks. Use 1/3 cup sauce mix and 1 cup water in saucepan to make white sauce or gravy. Simmer over medium heat until thickened, stirring constantly; do not boil. May substitute low-sodium chicken or beef broth for water.

Approx Per Tablespoon: Cal 27; Prot 2.1 g; Carbo 4.4 g; T Fat 0.1 g; Chol 0.0 mg; Potas 96.5 mg; Sod 26.7 mg.

Connie Winter, Kentucky

FAUX MAYO

1 tablespoon cornstarch
1 cup cold water
2 tablespoons olive oil
2 tablespoons low-fat yogurt
2 tablespoons white vinegar
1 teaspoon prepared mustard
1/2 teaspoon prepared
horseradish

Yield: 16 tablespoons

Combine cornstarch and cold water in saucepan; mix well. Bring to a boil over medium heat, stirring constantly. Cool for 1 to 2 minutes or until mixture is translucent. Pour into small bowl. Mix in olive oil, yogurt, vinegar, mustard and horseradish. Store, covered, in refrigerator for up to 2 weeks. May add 1 tablespoon low-sodium catsup and dash of hot pepper sauce.

Approx Per Tablespoon: Cal 18; Prot 0.1 g; Carbo 0.7 g; T Fat 1.7 g; Chol 0.1 mg; Potas 3.1 mg; Sod 0.1 mg.

Miriam Bates, Minnesota

HALF-HOUR APPLE BUTTER

2 cups unsweetened applesauce
1/2 cup (or less) sugar
1 teaspoon cinnamon
1/4 teaspoon allspice
1/8 teaspoon ginger
1/8 teaspoon cloves

Yield: 4 servings

Combine applesauce, sugar and spices in saucepan; mix well. Bring to a boil. Cook for 30 minutes, stirring frequently.

Approx Per Serving: Cal 149; Prot 0.2 g;
Carbo 38.6 g; T Fat 0.1 g; Chol 0.0 mg;
Potas 92.4 mg; Sod 3.1 mg.

Joyce Engle, Indiana

PEACHY BERRY CONSERVE

1 10-ounce package frozen
sweetened strawberries, thawed
1 cup drained canned peaches
1/2 teaspoon ascorbic acid
1 package powdered fruit
pectin
1/2 cup water
3 cups sugar
1/4 cup water
1/4 cup slivered almonds
1 tablespoon grated lemon rind

Yield: 64 tablespoons

Combine strawberries and peaches in bowl. Sprinkle with ascorbic acid. Let stand for 20 minutes. Combine pectin and 1/2 cup water in saucepan. Bring to a boil, stirring constantly. Boil for 1 minute, stirring constantly. Remove from heat. Add sugar and 1/4 cup water; mix well. Stir in almonds and lemon rind. Pour mixture into hot sterilized jars; seal with 2-piece lids. Cool. Store in refrigerator.

Approx Per Tablespoon: Cal 46; Prot 0.1 g;
Carbo 11.4 g; T Fat 0.3 g; Chol 0.0 mg;
Potas 13.3 mg; Sod 0.2 mg.

Janice Jett, Illinois

HOLIDAY FRUIT COMPOTE

3 10-ounce packages frozen
sliced peaches
4 cups frozen whole
strawberries
4 cups frozen Bing cherries
1 20-ounce can pineapple
slices
2 20-ounce cans pineapple
chunks
5 bananas, sliced diagonally
2 11-ounce cans mandarin
oranges
1 cup shredded coconut

Yield: 30 servings

Thaw frozen fruit; drain all fruit. Layer pineapple slices, pineapple chunks, peaches, strawberries, cherries, bananas, mandarin oranges and coconut in large serving bowl. Chill for 3 or 4 hours. Coat bananas with ascorbic acid to prevent browning.

Approx Per Serving: Cal 155; Prot 1.2 g;
Carbo 37.3 g; T Fat 1.4 g; Chol 0.0 mg;
Potas 296.0 mg; Sod 12.8 mg.

Edna Smithson, Delaware

Breads

BREADS

One of the biggest revelations to have hit the food and health scene in the past few years is the importance of fiber in a healthy diet. Not that fiber has ever been a secret. But until recent advances in medical research, the importance of this common food was underplayed.

Now we know that a high-fiber, low-fat diet is one of the very best ways to reduce the risk of colon cancer while lowering blood cholesterol levels. One of the easiest ways to put fiber in the diet is in the form of bran, the cracked outer shell of grains.

Until about 1989, wheat bran was the best known, but the hottest new "miracle drug" on the nutrition scene is oat bran, which may really be something of a wonder. A mere 50 to 100 grams a day (about 1/3 to 2/3 cup) of oat bran can reduce your blood cholesterol by an amazing 3 to 15 percent. Wheat bran, rice bran and corn bran, while perhaps not as dramatic, also lay claim to healthful benefits.

If you like to bake but have never tried dark or whole grain flours, now is the time to start. Flour products are better than ever, more widely available, and no harder to work with than more processed flours.

The recipes we've collected in the following chapter include a good variety of both yeast and quick breads, rolls and biscuits using both white and whole-grain flours. Try making several at a time, and serve a basket of homemade treats today while you tuck some in the freezer for another occasion.

In baking yeast breads, keep in mind that you can still make a few substitutions that can save calories, fat and cholesterol, though perhaps not as easily as in other foods. Use a nonstick spray for greasing pans, not butter or margarine. Use margarine, not butter, in recipes, and skim milk in place of whole milk.

Until very recently, sugar substitutes, such as saccharine and aspartame, were not of great help in baking, because they lost their sweetening qualities when exposed to high heats. A new product, Sunette, can be used for baking, keeping in mind that you should still use about half of the sugar called for in a recipe, as it often influences such factors as browning and crispness.

Whatever ingredients you choose, one of the nicest things about making bread at home is the knowledge that something so much fun to work with and so good to eat can be so good for you.

ANGEL BISCUITS

1 package dry yeast
2 tablespoons lukewarm water
5 to 5½ cups sifted flour
1 teaspoon soda
3 teaspoons baking powder
¼ cup sugar
1 teaspoon salt
1 cup shortening
2 cups buttermilk

Yield: 48 servings

Dissolve yeast in water in small bowl. Sift flour, soda, baking powder, sugar and salt in large bowl. Cut in shortening until crumbly. Add yeast and buttermilk; mix well. Knead dough on floured surface until smooth and elastic. Roll to ½ to ¾-inch thickness. Cut with biscuit cutter. Fold each biscuit in half; place on baking sheet. Bake for 15 to 20 minutes or until golden brown.

Approx Per Serving: Cal 95; Prot 1.8 g; Carbo 11.7 g; T Fat 4.5 g; Chol 0.4 mg; Potas 31.2 mg; Sod 93.2 mg.

Hayden Rorke, Alabama

BUTTERMILK BISCUITS

2 cups flour
4 teaspoons baking powder
½ teaspoon soda
½ teaspoon salt
5 tablespoons shortening
1 cup buttermilk

Yield: 24 biscuits

Sift flour, baking powder, soda and salt into bowl. Cut in shortening until crumbly. Add buttermilk; mix until dough follows fork. Knead for 30 seconds on floured surface. Roll to ¼-inch thickness. Brush with oil. Fold dough in half. Cut double biscuits with small biscuit cutter. Place on ungreased baking sheet. Bake at 450 degrees for 12 to 15 minutes or until light brown.

Approx Per Biscuit: Cal 67; Prot 1.4 g; Carbo 8.6 g; T Fat 2.9 g; Chol 0.4 mg; Potas 26.2 mg; Sod 127.0 mg.

Joy Delight, Oklahoma

WHOLE WHEAT BREADSTICKS

1 cup whole wheat flour
1 teaspoon cinnamon
1 teaspoon soda
¼ cup margarine
¾ cup shredded Cheddar cheese
1 egg, beaten
1 teaspoon cold milk

Yield: 24 breadsticks

Mix flour with cinnamon and soda in bowl. Cut in margarine and cheese with pastry blender until crumbly. Add mixture of egg and milk; mix with fork until mixture forms ball. Shape by teaspoonfuls into sticks. Place 1 inch apart on ungreased baking sheet. Bake at 375 degrees for 8 to 10 minutes or until light brown. May shape into larger sticks and increase baking time.

Approx Per Breadstick: Cal 52; Prot 1.8 g; Carbo 3.7 g; T Fat 3.4 g; Chol 15.2 mg; Potas 26.5 mg; Sod 81.7 mg.

Opal Harrison, Texas

ANGEL CORNSTICKS

1 package dry yeast
1¹/₂ cups cornmeal
1 cup flour
1 tablespoon sugar
1¹/₂ teaspoons baking powder
¹/₂ teaspoon soda
1 teaspoon salt
2 eggs, beaten
2 cups buttermilk
¹/₂ cup oil

Yield: 36 cornsticks

Combine yeast, cornmeal, flour, sugar, baking powder, soda and salt in large bowl. Beat eggs with buttermilk and oil in large bowl. Add to dry ingredients; stir until smooth. Fill greased cast-iron cornstick pans ¹/₂ full. Bake at 450 degrees for 12 to 15 minutes or until golden brown.

Approx Per Cornstick: Cal 72; Prot 1.7 g; Carbo 8.3 g; T Fat 3.6 g; Chol 15.7 mg; Potas 38.6 mg; Sod 102.0 mg.

Felice Fowler, New Hampshire

MEXICAN CORN BREAD

1 cup self-rising cornmeal
¹/₂ teaspoon red pepper
¹/₂ cup chopped onion
¹/₂ cup chopped green bell pepper
¹/₂ cup shredded low-fat Cheddar cheese
1 cup skim milk
2 eggs, beaten
1   8¹/₂-ounce can cream-style corn

Yield: 16 servings

Combine cornmeal and red pepper in bowl. Add remaining ingredients; mix well. Spoon into 8x8-inch baking pan sprayed with nonstick cooking spray. Bake at 450 degrees for 25 minutes or until golden brown. Cut into 2-inch squares.

Approx Per Serving: Cal 70; Prot 3.2 g; Carbo 9.8 g; T Fat 2.3 g; Chol 38.2 mg; Potas 93.8 mg; Sod 81.7 mg.

Arthur White, Arizona

YEAST CORN BREAD

1¹/₄ cups yellow cornmeal
4 cups boiling water
1 cup molasses
1 tablespoon margarine
2 tablespoons sugar
1 teaspoon salt
1 package yeast
¹/₄ cup warm water
2 cups (about) flour

Yield: 40 servings

Stir cornmeal into boiling water in saucepan. Cook until smooth; remove from heat. Stir in molasses, margarine, sugar and salt. Cool. Dissolve yeast in ¹/₄ cup warm water. Add to cornmeal mixture. Add enough flour to make a stiff dough; mix well. Let rise for 1 hour. Punch dough down. Let rise until doubled in bulk. Shape into 4 loaves. Place in loaf pans. Bake at 350 degrees for 1 hour.

Approx Per Serving: Cal 59; Prot 1.1 g; Carbo 12.7 g; T Fat 0.5 g; Chol 0.0 mg; Potas 255.0 mg; Sod 63.6 mg.

Renee Smith, Montana

SPOON BREAD

1 cup yellow cornmeal
1/3 cup water
1 cup hominy grits
3 cups water
1/4 cup margarine
1 egg, slightly beaten
1/2 cup evaporated milk
1/2 cup water
1 teaspoon baking powder

Yield: 12 servings

Combine cornmeal and 1/3 cup water in bowl; mix well. Let stand for several minutes. Cook grits in 3 cups water in saucepan over medium heat for 15 minutes or until thickened, stirring constantly. Stir in margarine until melted. Cool. Add to cornmeal mixture; mix well. Add egg, evaporated milk mixed with 1/2 cup water, baking powder and salt to taste. Pour into greased 9x9-inch loaf pan. Place in larger pan of water. Bake at 350 degrees for 60 to 75 minutes or until brown. Reduce temperature if spoon bread browns too fast.

Approx Per Serving: Cal 139; Prot 3.3 g; Carbo 18.9 g; T Fat 5.7 g; Chol 26.0 mg; Potas 85.1 mg; Sod 49.3 mg.

Wilma Randolph, Maine

OAT BRAN BREAD

1 cup oat bran
1 1/2 cups boiling water
2 packages dry yeast
1/2 cup warm (105 to
115-degree) water
1/4 cup oil
1/4 cup honey
1 1/2 teaspoons salt
4 1/2 to 5 cups flour
1 egg white
2 tablespoons oat bran

Yield: 24 servings

Combine 1 cup oat bran and boiling water in bowl; mix well. Set aside to cool. Dissolve yeast in warm water in large bowl. Stir in oat bran mixture, oil, honey, salt and 2 cups flour. Beat until smooth. Stir in enough remaining flour to make a soft dough. Knead on lightly floured surface for 8 to 10 minutes or until smooth and elastic. Place in greased bowl, turning to grease surface. Let rise, covered, in warm place for 30 minutes or until doubled in bulk. Punch dough down; divide into 2 portions. Roll each portion into 8x12-inch rectangle on floured surface. Roll up from narrow end. Place seam side down in greased 5x9-inch loaf pans. Let rise, covered, in warm place for 30 minutes or until doubled in bulk. Brush with egg white. Sprinkle with 2 tablespoons oat bran. Bake at 375 degrees for 35 minutes or until loaves test done. Remove to wire rack to cool.

Approx Per Serving: Cal 138; Prot 3.9 g; Carbo 25.9 g; T Fat 2.7 g; Chol 0.0 mg; Potas 64.0 mg; Sod 137.0 mg.

Mildred Nash, Oklahoma

MILK AND HONEY BREAD

2 packages dry yeast
3 cups warm (105 to
115-degree) water
1/2 cup honey
1/2 cup oil
1 teaspoon salt
2 cups nonfat dry milk powder
7 to 8 cups whole wheat flour

Yield: 36 servings

Dissolve yeast in water in bowl. Add honey, oil and salt; mix well. Add dry milk powder and 3 cups flour; mix well. Add enough remaining flour to make medium dough. Knead on floured surface until smooth and elastic. Place in greased bowl, turning to grease surface. Let rise, covered, for 45 minutes or until doubled in bulk. Divide dough into 3 portions. Shape into loaves. Place in greased 5x9-inch loaf pans. Let rise until doubled in bulk. Bake at 350 degrees for 30 minutes. Remove to wire rack to cool.

Approx Per Serving: Cal 145; Prot 5.0 g; Carbo 24.9 g; T Fat 3.6 g; Chol 0.7 mg; Potas 173.0 mg; Sod 80.8 mg.

Leslie Wyatt, Iowa

SPICE BREAD-IN-A-JAR

2/3 cup shortening
22/3 cups sugar
2 cups applesauce
2/3 cup water
4 eggs
31/3 cups flour
2 teaspoons soda
1/2 teaspoon baking powder
11/2 teaspoons salt
1 teaspoon cinnamon
1 teaspoon cloves
1 cup chopped walnuts
1 cup raisins

Yield: 56 servings

Cream shortening and sugar in mixer bowl until light and fluffy. Add applesauce, water and eggs; mix well. Add mixture of flour, soda, baking powder, salt and spices; mix well. Stir in walnuts and raisins. Spray 7 wide-mouthed 1-pint jars with nonstick cooking spray. Fill jars 2/3 full. Bake at 325 degrees for exactly 45 minutes. Remove jars from oven 1 at a time and seal quickly with 2-piece lids, pressing bread down if necessary. Let stand until cool. Give as gifts. Use only jars suitable for canning.

Approx Per Serving: Cal 120; Prot 1.6 g; Carbo 19.7 g; T Fat 4.3 g; Chol 19.6 mg; Potas 50.8 mg; Sod 3.6 mg.

Lenora Byford, Florida

COFFEE CAN ENGLISH MUFFIN BREAD

1 package dry yeast
1/2 cup warm (105 to 115-
degree) water
4 teaspoons sugar
2 tablespoons oil
1 13-ounce can evaporated
milk
1 teaspoon salt
4 cups flour

Yield: 20 slices

Dissolve yeast in warm water in large mixer bowl. Add 1 teaspoon sugar. Let stand for 15 minutes or until bubbly. Add remaining sugar, oil, evaporated milk and salt. Add 3 cups flour 1 cup at a time, beating well at low speed after each addition. Stir in remaining 1 cup flour. Divide dough between 2 well-greased 1-pound coffee cans; cover with well-greased plastic lids. Let rise until lids pop off. Bake, uncovered, at 350 degrees for 40 to 60 minutes or until loaves test done. Remove from cans immediately. Serve hot or toasted.

Approx Per Slice: Cal 132; Prot 4.0 g;
Carbo 21.8 g; T Fat 3.1 g; Chol 5.4 mg;
Potas 86.7 mg; Sod 126.7 mg.

Sandra Boucher, Kentucky

SOUTHWEST VIRGINIA BROWN BREAD

1 cup packed brown sugar
1 cup dark molasses
3 packages dry yeast
2 teaspoons salt
2 cups instant dry milk powder
7 cups warm (105 to
115-degree) water
5 tablespoons melted
shortening
3 eggs, slightly beaten
9 cups whole wheat flour
8 to 9 cups all-purpose flour

Yield: 60 slices

Combine brown sugar, molasses, yeast, salt and dry milk powder in large bowl. Add water, shortening, eggs and whole wheat flour; mix well. Let stand for 15 minutes. Add enough all-purpose flour to make slightly sticky but elastic dough. Knead on floured surface for 7 minutes. Place in greased bowl, turning to coat surface. Let rise, covered, until doubled in bulk. Punch dough down. Let rise again until doubled in bulk. Shape into loaves; place in greased loaf pans. Let rise until more than doubled in bulk. Bake at 350 degrees for 45 minutes or until loaves test done. Makes wonderful toast and peanut butter and jelly sandwiches.

Approx Per Slice: Cal 176; Prot 5.6 g;
Carbo 34.9 g; T Fat 1.9 g; Chol 14.1 mg;
Potas 302.0 mg; Sod 94.9 mg.

Rick Miller, Washington, D.C.

Apple and Oat Bran Muffins

2 cups oat bran cereal
1/4 cup packed brown sugar
1 tablespoon baking powder
1 cup skim milk
2 egg whites, slightly beaten
1 cup chopped apple
1/2 cup chopped pecans
1/2 cup raisins

Yield: 18 muffins

Spray bottom of muffin cups with nonstick cooking spray. Combine first 5 ingredients in bowl; mix until moistened. Stir in apple, pecans and raisins. Spoon into muffin cups. Let stand for 3 to 4 minutes before placing in oven. Bake at 425 degrees for 17 minutes or until lightly browned.

Approx Per Muffin: Cal 82; Prot 3.1 g; Carbo 16.0 g; T Fat 2.7 g; Chol 0.2 mg; Potas 150.0 mg; Sod 71.8 mg.

Charmet Stephenson, Tennessee

Whole Wheat Apple Muffins

1 cup oats
1 cup whole wheat pastry flour
1 teaspoon baking powder
1/2 teaspoon soda
1/4 teaspoon salt
1/4 teaspoon cinnamon
1/4 teaspoon nutmeg
1 cup (rounded) chopped apples
1 cup plain yogurt
1/4 cup honey
2 tablespoons oil

Yield: 12 muffins

Combine oats, flour, baking powder, soda, salt, cinnamon and nutmeg in bowl; mix well. Add mixture of apples, yogurt, honey and oil; stir just until moistened. Fill greased muffin cups 3/4 full. Bake at 400 degrees for 15 to 20 minutes or until muffins test done. Remove to wire rack to cool.

Approx Per Muffin: Cal 119; Prot 3.5 g; Carbo 20.2 g; T Fat 3.2 g; Chol 1.2 mg; Potas 119.0 mg; Sod 120.1 mg.

Lucy Jones, Iowa

Banana Muffins

3 eggs
1 cup packed brown sugar
1 cup sugar
1 cup oil
1 teaspoon vanilla extract
1 1/2 cups buttermilk
1 1/2 cups mashed bananas
3 cups flour
3 cups unprocessed bran
1 tablespoon baking powder
1 tablespoon soda
1 teaspoon salt
1 cup raisins

Yield: 48 muffins

Combine eggs, brown sugar, sugar, oil, vanilla, buttermilk and bananas in mixer bowl; mix well. Add mixture of flour, bran, baking powder, soda and salt, mixing just until moistened. Stir in raisins gently. Let stand for 30 minutes. Fill greased muffin cups 2/3 full. Bake at 350 degrees for 20 minutes or until brown.

Approx Per Muffin: Cal 132; Prot 2.0 g; Carbo 20.7 g; T Fat 5.2 g; Chol 17.4 mg; Potas 119.0 mg; Sod 132.0 mg.

Zelma Long, Minnesota

Whole Wheat Bran Muffins

1 cup whole wheat flour
1 teaspoon soda
1/2 cup whole bran
1 egg
1/2 cup dark molasses
3/4 cup milk
2 teaspoons margarine, softened
1/2 cup golden raisins
1/2 cup chopped pecans

Yield: 24 muffins

Mix whole wheat flour, soda, whole bran, egg, molasses, milk and margarine in mixer bowl; mix well. Stir in raisins and pecans. Spoon into paper-lined muffin cups. Bake at 350 degrees for 15 to 20 minutes or until muffins test done.

Approx Per Muffin: Cal 70; Prot 1.6 g; Carbo 11.2 g; T Fat 2.6 g; Chol 12.4 mg; Potas 271.0 mg; Sod 50.0 mg.

Roberta Roberts, California

Popovers

2 eggs, slightly beaten
1 cup flour
1 cup milk
1/2 teaspoon salt

Yield: 12 popovers

Preheat oven to 450 degrees. Combine eggs, flour, milk and salt in bowl; mix just until moistened. Fill greased muffin cups 3/4 full. Reduce temperature to 350 degrees. Bake for 20 minutes or until golden brown.

Approx Per Popover: Cal 64; Prot 2.8 g; Carbo 9.0 g; T Fat 1.7 g; Chol 48.4 mg; Potas 48.0 mg; Sod 109.0 mg.

Genevieve Marpelsky, Wyoming

Healthy Pancake Mix

3/4 cup all-purpose flour
1/4 cup whole wheat flour
1/2 cup ground oats
1/4 cup buttermilk powder
2 tablespoons sugar
1 1/2 teaspoons baking powder
1/2 teaspoon soda
1/4 teaspoon salt
1 cup water
3 tablespoons oil
2 eggs, slightly beaten

Yield: 12 pancakes

Combine all-purpose flour, whole wheat flour, oats, buttermilk powder, sugar, baking powder, soda and salt in bowl; mix well. Store in airtight container until ready to use. To prepare pancakes, combine water, oil and eggs in bowl; mix well. Add pancake mix; mix well. Ladle 1/4 cup batter into lightly greased skillet. Cook for 3 to 4 minutes, turning once. Serve immediately. This easy, make-ahead mix makes a great gift with assorted syrups or preserves. Oat bran cereal can be substituted for the ground oats.

Approx Per Pancake: Cal 111; Prot 3.6 g; Carbo 13.5 g; T Fat 4.8 g; Chol 47.4 mg; Potas 79.9 mg; Sod 145.0 mg.

Louise Merrell, Indiana

No-Cholesterol Pancakes

2 cups flour
1/4 cup sugar
4 teaspoons baking powder
4 egg whites
2 cups nonfat milk
1/2 cup oil

Yield: 12 pancakes

Combine flour, sugar and baking powder in bowl; mix well. Add egg whites, milk and oil; mix well. Pour batter 1/4 cup at a time onto hot greased griddle. Bake until brown on both sides.

Approx Per Pancake: Cal 193; Prot 4.7 g; Carbo 22.4 g; T Fat 4.7 g; Chol 0.4 mg; Potas 52.5 mg; Sod 325.0 mg.

Grace Wahlgren, Colorado

Swedish Oatmeal Pancakes

4 cups rolled oats
1 cup flour
1/4 cup sugar
2 teaspoons soda
2 teaspoons baking powder
1/8 teaspoon salt
1 quart buttermilk
4 eggs, beaten
1/2 cup melted margarine
2 teaspoons vanilla extract

Yield: 27 pancakes

Combine first 6 ingredients in large bowl. Add buttermilk, eggs, margarine and vanilla; mix well. Let stand for 30 to 45 minutes or until batter has thickened to desired consistency. Ladle onto hot buttered griddle. Bake until puffed and brown on both sides, turning once. Serve with warm spiced applesauce and sour cream or peanut butter and applesauce. Store cooled pancakes between waxed paper in refrigerator and reheat in microwave.

Approx Per Pancake: Cal 127; Prot 4.6 g; Carbo 15.2 g; T Fat 5.4 g; Chol 41.9 mg; Potas 112.0 mg; Sod 148.0 mg.

Roberta Hull, Washington

Gingerbread Waffles

3 cups flour
1 teaspoon soda
1 teaspoon baking powder
1/2 teaspoon salt
1 teaspoon ginger
1/2 teaspoon cinnamon
1/4 teaspoon cloves
3 eggs, beaten
1/4 cup sugar
1/2 cup molasses
1 cup buttermilk
5 1/3 tablespoons melted shortening

Yield: 6 waffles

Sift flour, soda, baking powder, salt, ginger, cinnamon and cloves together. Beat eggs until light. Add sugar, molasses and buttermilk; mix well. Add sifted dry ingredients; beat until smooth. Mix in shortening. Bake in preheated waffle iron according to manufacturer's instructions. Serve with hot honey and whipped cream.

Approx Per Waffle: Cal 474; Prot 10.9 g; Carbo 72.9 g; T Fat 15.2 g; Chol 138.0 mg; Potas 936.0 mg; Sod 473.0 mg.

William Bentson, Ohio

SOFT PRETZELS

1 package dry yeast
1½ cups warm (105 to
115-degree) water
4 cups flour
1½ teaspoons sugar
¼ teaspoon salt
1 egg, beaten
Coarse salt to taste

Yield: 24 pretzels

Dissolve yeast in water in bowl. Add flour, sugar and ¼ teaspoon salt; mix well. Knead on floured surface until smooth and elastic. Shape into pretzels on baking sheet. Brush with egg. Sprinkle with coarse salt. Bake at 350 degrees for 15 minutes or until brown.

Approx Per Pretzel: Cal 81; Prot 2.5 g; Carbo 16.2 g; T Fat 0.4 g; Chol 11.4 mg; Potas 28.5 mg; Sod 46.6 mg.

Nicole Rusk, Georgia

VERSATILE DINNER ROLLS

1 package dry yeast
2 tablespoons warm (105 to
115-degree) water
1 cup hot milk
7 tablespoons margarine
2 tablespoons honey
2 tablespoons sugar
1 teaspoon salt
2 eggs, slightly beaten
4 cups flour

Yield: 24 rolls

Dissolve yeast in warm water. Combine next 5 ingredients in mixer bowl; mix well. Stir in eggs, yeast and 2 cups flour. Stir in remaining flour. Place in greased bowl, turning to grease surface. Chill, covered, for 2 hours or longer. Shape into rolls in greased 10x15-inch pan. Let rise until doubled in bulk. Bake at 400 degrees for 15 minutes or until golden brown.

Approx Per Roll: Cal 129; Prot 3.2 g; Carbo 19.0 g; T Fat 4.3 g; Chol 24.2 mg; Potas 47.4 mg; Sod 139.0 mg.

Viola Gunter, Massachusetts

OATMEAL ROLLS

1 package dry yeast
⅓ cup warm (105 to
110-degree) water
1 cup quick-cooking oats
1 cup milk
1 cup water
3 tablespoons melted
shortening
1 teaspoon salt
⅓ cup packed brown sugar
4½ cups sifted flour

Yield: 36 rolls

Dissolve yeast in ⅓ cup warm water. Combine milk and 1 cup water in saucepan. Bring just to the boiling point. Pour over oats in bowl. Cool to lukewarm. Stir in shortening, salt and brown sugar. Add yeast; mix well. Stir in flour. Knead on lightly floured surface until smooth and elastic. Place in greased bowl, turning to grease surface. Let rise, covered, until doubled in bulk. Shape into desired rolls. Place on baking sheet. Let rise until doubled in bulk. Bake at 350 degrees for 15 minutes or until lightly browned.

Approx Per Roll: Cal 83; Prot 2.2 g; Carbo 14.8 g; T Fat 1.6 g; Chol 0.9 mg; Potas 41.4 mg; Sod 63.0 mg.

Ellen Cole, New York

Herb Rolls

1/4 cup margarine, melted
1 1/2 teaspoons parsley
3 tablespoons Parmesan cheese
1/2 teaspoon dillseed
1   10-count can refrigerator
    buttermilk biscuits

Yield: 20 small rolls

Combine first 4 ingredients in baking pan. Cut biscuits in half. Coat with margarine mixture. Arrange in 9-inch pan with sides touching. Bake at 425 degrees for 12 to 15 minutes.

Approx Per Roll: Cal 57; Prot 1.1 g; Carbo 4.9 g; T Fat 3.6 g; Chol 1.1 mg; Potas 12.4 mg; Sod 165.0 mg.

Adrienne Kirk, California

Mini Cinnamon Rolls

1   8-count package refrigerator
    crescent rolls
1/4 cup margarine, softened
2 teaspoons cinnamon
4 teaspoons sugar
1/2 cup raisins
1 cup confectioners' sugar
2 tablespoons milk

Yield: 24 rolls

Separate rolls into 4 rectangles. Press perforations to seal. Spread with margarine. Sprinkle with mixture of cinnamon and sugar. Top with raisins. Roll up rectangles. Cut each into 6 slices. Arrange in 9-inch baking dish. Bake at 375 degrees for 17 to 23 minutes or until golden brown. Drizzle with mixture of confectioners' sugar and milk. Serve warm.

Approx Per Roll: Cal 76; Prot 0.8 g; Carbo 12.4 g; T Fat 2.6 g; Chol 0.2 mg; Potas 41.7 mg; Sod 75.1 mg.

Andrew Markey, North Dakota

Wheat Pita Bread

1 package dry yeast
3 cups whole wheat flour
1 teaspoon salt
1 1/2 teaspoons sugar
2 1/2 cups warm (105 to
    115-degree) water
2 tablespoons oil
3 cups whole wheat flour

Yield: 24 pitas

Combine first 4 ingredients in mixer bowl; mix well. Add water and oil. Beat at low speed until moistened. Beat at medium speed for 3 minutes. Add remaining flour by hand to make stiff dough. Knead on floured surface for 10 minutes or until smooth and elastic. Cover with plastic wrap and a towel. Let rise for 20 minutes. Punch dough down. Divide into 4 portions. Divide each portion into 6 pieces. Shape pieces into balls. Roll balls into 5-inch circles on lightly floured surface. Place on baking sheet. Let rise, covered, for 30 minutes. Bake at 500 degrees for 5 minutes or until puffed and tops just begin to brown. Remove to wire rack to cool.

Approx Per Pita: Cal 112; Prot 4.1 g; Carbo 21.7 g; T Fat 1.7 g; Chol 0.0 mg; Potas 117.0 mg; Sod 90.3 mg.

Jean Williams, Iowa

Desserts

DESSERTS

Not only can desserts be non-harmful to your health—they can actually be beneficial. We don't just mean in the psychological sense, as you slip into a chocolate-induced haze of bliss after dinner. We mean really good for you, as in fresh fruit, low-fat ices and puddings and high-fiber cookies.

In preparing desserts, keep an eye out for places where, once again, a low-fat or low-sugar variation of an ingredient can be substituted, e.g. Neufchâtel cheese for cream cheese, evaporated skim milk for heavy cream, ice milk or frozen yogurt for ice cream, brown sugar substitute for brown sugar.

Whenever possible, use egg whites instead of whole eggs, a great way to cut cholesterol, or use egg substitute. Raisins are a good substitute for nuts in many desserts and have no fat. As is the case with breads, most sugar substitutes will work fine in uncooked foods, but lose their sweetness when subjected to high heat. A new product, Sunette, will work in baked goods, but you should retain at least half of the sugar called for in a recipe, as it affects crispness and browning.

In many cases where canned or dried fruit are listed as an ingredient, fresh fruit makes a good substitute. If a syrup is needed, make one with low-cal sweetener instead of sugar. Remember to use nonstick vegetable oil spray to grease pans instead of butter or margarine; use margarine instead of butter; and try to replace half the fat in a recipe with a slightly larger amount of another liquid, such as fruit juice, plain yogurt or applesauce. Experiment to see what works.

For summer, try your hand at homemade fruit sorbets and ices, either using one of the new small, hand-turned ice cream makers or simply ice cube trays. A basket of fresh fruit offers a world of possibilities that needs little more than a touch of honey or lemon juice to become elegant desserts. In winter, frozen berries puréed with just a touch of orange juice and poured over vanilla ice milk is a special treat that's easy on the diet.

You'll find ample cookie recipes in the chapter that follows, both delicate and stick-to-your-ribs varieties, delectable cakes of every description, and many other elegant and health-conscious endings to your memorable meals.

BAKED APPLE AND STRAWBERRY COMPOTE

1 cup sliced strawberries
1¹/₂ teaspoons Sherry extract
¹/₂ teaspoon cinnamon
8 packets artificial sweetener
3 cups sliced strawberries
4 apples, peeled, sliced

Yield: 4 servings

Combine 1 cup strawberries, flavoring, cinnamon and sweetener in blender container; process until smooth. Combine remaining 3 cups strawberries and apples in 9x9-inch baking dish. Pour strawberry purée over fruit; toss lightly to coat. Bake at 375 degrees for 30 minutes or until apples are tender.

Approx Per Serving: Cal 119; Prot 1.1 g; Carbo 29.5 g; T Fat 1.0 g; Chol 0.0 mg; Potas 392.0 mg; Sod 2.2 mg.

Ruth Webb, Oklahoma

APPLE TURNOVERS

3 apples, chopped
6 tablespoons plus 2 teaspoons unsweetened apple juice concentrate
¹/₂ teaspoon cinnamon
2 teaspoons cornstarch
¹/₂ teaspoon nutmeg
1 8-count package refrigerator crescent rolls
4 teaspoons confectioners' sugar
¹/₂ teaspoon water

Yield: 8 servings

Combine apples, juice concentrate, cinnamon, cornstarch and nutmeg in glass bowl; mix well. Microwave on High for 16 minutes, stirring every 4 minutes. Separate dough into triangles. Pat each triangle slightly larger. Divide filling into 8 portions. Spoon onto dough. Fold dough over filling to make triangles. Press edges with fork to seal. Place on baking sheet. Bake at 350 degrees for 10 minutes. Drizzle with mixture of confectioners' sugar and water.

Approx Per Serving: Cal 143; Prot 1.4 g; Carbo 24.5 g; T Fat 4.8 g; Chol 0.0 mg; Potas 177.0 mg; Sod 195.0 mg.

Mazzie Kimberly, Georgia

BAKED HONEY BANANAS

6 bananas
2 tablespoons melted margarine
2 tablespoons lemon juice
¹/₄ cup honey

Yield: 12 servings

Cut bananas in half lengthwise. Arrange in 9x13-inch baking dish. Combine margarine, lemon juice and honey in bowl. Drizzle mixture over bananas. Bake at 325 degrees for 15 minutes, turning occasionally.

Approx Per Serving: Cal 91; Prot 0.6 g; Carbo 19.3 g; T Fat 2.2 g; Chol 0.0 mg; Potas 232.0 mg; Sod 17.5 mg.

Willis Harmon, Texas

Vanilla Cheesecake with Strawberries

1 3-ounce package ladyfingers
2 tablespoons cornstarch
1/4 cup water
15 ounces part-skim ricotta cheese
1 teaspoon vanilla extract
3 tablespoons sugar
2 tablespoons lemon juice
1 cup plain nonfat yogurt
2 egg whites, stiffly beaten
4 cups fresh strawberries
1 tablespoon sugar

Yield: 8 servings

Spray 7-inch springform pan with nonstick cooking spray. Trim 1/2 inch from bottoms of ladyfingers. Arrange cut sides down around sides of prepared pan. Dissolve cornstarch in water. Combine with ricotta, vanilla, 3 tablespoons sugar, lemon juice and yogurt in food processor container. Process until smooth. Pour into bowl. Fold in egg whites gently. Pour into prepared pan. Bake for 1 hour and 15 minutes or until almost set in center. Let stand for 1 hour. Chill, tightly covered, overnight. Reserve 5 whole strawberries for garnish. Purée remaining strawberries in blender container. Add 1 tablespoon sugar. Process until mixed. Arrange reserved strawberries over top of cheesecake. Serve with sauce.

Approx Per Serving: Cal 177; Prot 10 g; Carbo 24 g; T Fat 5 g; Chol 43 mg; Sod 128 mg.

Photograph for this recipe is on the cover.

Peach Ice Cream

2 tablespoons unflavored gelatin
3 cups milk
2 cups sugar
1/4 teaspoon salt
6 eggs
1 1/2 cups half and half
1 4-ounce package vanilla instant pudding mix
5 teaspoons vanilla extract
4 cups crushed peaches

Yield: 16 servings

Soften gelatin in 1/2 cup milk. Scald 1 1/2 cups milk in saucepan. Stir in gelatin mixture until dissolved. Add remaining 1 cup milk, sugar and salt; mix well. Beat eggs in mixer bowl for 5 minutes. Add half and half, pudding mix, vanilla and gelatin mixture; mix well. Stir in peaches. Pour mixture into ice cream freezer container. Freeze according to manufacturer's instructions.

Approx Per Serving: Cal 233; Prot 6.3 g; Carbo 39.2 g; T Fat 6.3 g; Chol 117.0 mg; Potas 201.0 mg; Sod 134.0 mg.

Susan Woods, Nevada

SENSATIONAL ICE CREAM

6 egg whites
3/4 cup sugar
8 ounces whipped topping
1 teaspoon vanilla extract

Yield: 8 servings

Beat egg whites and salt to taste in mixer bowl until frothy. Add sugar 2 tablespoons at a time, beating constantly until stiff peaks form. Fold in whipped topping and vanilla gently. Pour into freezer container. Freeze for 4 hours or until serving time.

Approx Per Serving: Cal 175; Prot 2.9 g; Carbo 25.5 g; T Fat 7.2 g; Chol 0.0 mg; Potas 39.7 mg; Sod 45.2 mg.

Peggy Shaw, Illinois

ICEBERGS ON STICKS

8 ounces low-fat yogurt
Vanilla extract to taste
1 6-ounce can frozen orange
   juice concentrate

Yield: 5 servings

Combine yogurt, vanilla and orange juice concentrate in bowl; mix well. Fill 3-ounce paper cups 3/4 full. Freeze until slushy. Insert wooden sticks into cups for handles. Freeze until firm. Peel off paper cups to serve. This is an easy and healthy dessert or snack for children to make and eat. May substitute any unsweetened fruit juice concentrate for orange juice concentrate.

Approx Per Serving: Cal 83; Prot 3.2 g; Carbo 16.2 g; T Fat 0.8 g; Chol 2.8 mg; Potas 335.0 mg; Sod 32.7 mg.

Salina Mingus, Wyoming

QUICK PEACH COBBLER

1 cup flour
1/2 cup sugar
1 tablespoon baking powder
1/4 teaspoon cinnamon
2/3 cup milk
1 29-ounce can peaches
1/4 teaspoon nutmeg
1/4 teaspoon cinnamon

Yield: 8 servings

Combine flour, sugar, baking powder and 1/4 teaspoon cinnamon in bowl; mix well. Add milk; mix well. Pour into greased 9x13-inch baking dish. Heat peaches, nutmeg and 1/4 teaspoon cinnamon in saucepan. Spoon over batter. Bake at 350 degrees until golden brown.

Approx Per Serving: Cal 196; Prot 2.8 g; Carbo 46.1 g; T Fat 0.9 g; Chol 2.7 mg; Potas 139.0 mg; Sod 139.0 mg.

Judy Duncan, Alaska

MAPLED PEACHES

6 canned peach halves
6 teaspoons margarine
1/3 cup maple syrup
1/4 teaspoon cinnamon
1/8 teaspoon mace

Yield: 6 servings

Drain peaches reserving 1/3 cup syrup. Place peach halves cut side up in shallow 1-quart baking dish. Place 1 teaspoon margarine in each peach half. Combine maple syrup, cinnamon, mace and peach syrup in bowl; mix well. Pour over peaches. Bake at 375 degrees for 30 minutes.

Approx Per Serving: Cal 145; Prot 0.4 g; Carbo 29.4 g; T Fat 3.9 g; Chol 0.0 mg; Potas 105.0 mg; Sod 53.2 mg.

Traci Duane, North Dakota

PECAN CUPS

1/2 cup margarine, softened
1 cup flour
3 ounces cream cheese, softened
3/4 cup packed brown sugar
1 egg
1 tablespoon melted margarine
1/8 teaspoon vanilla extract
1 cup chopped pecans

Yield: 36 cups

Mix first 3 ingredients in small bowl. Shape into log. Chill, tightly wrapped, for 3 hours. Divide into 3 portions. Cut each into 12 slices. Press each slice into muffin cup. Combine brown sugar, egg, melted margarine, vanilla and pecans in medium bowl; mix well. Spoon a small amount of brown sugar mixture into prepared muffin cups. Bake at 375 degrees for 15 to 20 minutes or until lightly browned.

Approx Per Cup: Cal 88; Prot 1.0 g; Carbo 7.8 g; T Fat 6.1 g; Chol 10.2 mg; Potas 38.2 mg; Sod 44.5 mg.

Lorrie Joyce, Illinois

PINEAPPLE-ORANGE DESSERT

1 3-ounce package tapioca pudding mix
1 3-ounce package vanilla pudding and pie filling mix
3 cups cold water
1 3-ounce package orange gelatin
16 ounces whipped topping
1 16-ounce can mandarin oranges, drained
1 16-ounce can pineapple tidbits, drained

Yield: 20 servings

Combine tapioca pudding mix, pudding and pie filling mix and water in saucepan. Bring to a boil. Stir in gelatin. Cook until thickened, stirring constantly. Spoon into bowl. Chill for 2 hours or longer. Fold in whipped topping, oranges and pineapple. Chill until serving time.

Approx Per Serving: Cal 103; Prot 1.3 g; Carbo 19.6 g; T Fat 2.6 g; Chol 2.0 mg; Potas 68.0 mg; Sod 77.0 mg.

Pam Locher, Missouri

INDIAN PUDDING

2¹/₂ cups milk
3 tablespoons cornmeal
¹/₂ cup molasses
¹/₂ teaspoon cinnamon
¹/₄ teaspoon ginger

Yield: 8 servings

Heat milk in saucepan until tiny bubbles appear around edge. Add cornmeal 1 tablespoon at a time, mixing well after each addition. Stir in molasses. Cook over low heat for 10 to 15 minutes or until thickened, stirring frequently. Stir in cinnamon and ginger. Pour into greased baking dish. Bake at 300 degrees for 45 minutes.

Approx Per Serving: Cal 102; Prot 2.8 g; Carbo 17.1 g; T Fat 2.6 g; Chol 10.3 mg; Potas 289.0 mg; Sod 34.8 mg.

Sherry Jenks, Arkansas

RICE PUDDING

3 cups cooked rice
2 3-ounce packages vanilla instant pudding mix
1¹/₄ cups milk
1¹/₄ cups vanilla ice cream, softened
¹/₂ teaspoon cinnamon
2 cups whipped topping

Yield: 16 servings

Rinse rice with cool water after cooking; drain well. Combine pudding mix, milk, ice cream and cinnamon in mixer bowl. Beat for 1 minute. Fold in rice. Chill in refrigerator. Fold in whipped topping just before serving. Serve as side dish, salad or dessert.

Approx Per Serving: Cal 128; Prot 1.7 g; Carbo 22.0 g; T Fat 3.7 g; Chol 6.2 mg; Potas 52.2 mg; Sod 81.0 mg.

Pat McKinnie, South Dakota

APPLE FARM CAKE

¹/₄ cup shortening
1 cup sugar
1 egg
4 cups chopped apples
1 cup flour
1 teaspoon soda
1 teaspoon cinnamon
¹/₂ teaspoon nutmeg
¹/₄ teaspoon cloves

Yield: 16 servings

Cream shortening and sugar in mixer bowl until light and fluffy. Mix in egg and apples. Add mixture of sifted flour, soda and spices; mix well. Batter will be stiff. Spoon into greased 9x9-inch cake pan. Bake at 325 degrees for 45 minutes or until toothpick inserted in center comes out clean. Cut into squares while warm. Garnish with confectioners' sugar.

Approx Per Serving: Cal 127; Prot 1.3 g; Carbo 22.6 g; T Fat 1.0 g; Chol 17.1 mg; Potas 44.3 mg; Sod 56.4 mg.

Linda Howard, California

APPLE AND SPICE SNACK CAKE

1½ cups flour
¾ cup packed brown sugar
1 teaspoon soda
½ teaspoon allspice
1 cup chocolate chips
1 cup applesauce
⅓ cup oil
1 egg
⅔ cup apple juice
1 tablespoon lemon juice
1 teaspoon vanilla extract

Yield: 12 servings

Mix flour, brown sugar, soda and allspice in ungreased 9x9-inch baking pan. Sprinkle with chocolate chips. Combine applesauce, oil, egg, apple juice, lemon juice and vanilla in bowl; mix well. Add to dry ingredients in pan; stir until moistened. Bake at 350 degrees for 40 minutes.

Approx Per Serving: Cal 262; Prot 2.8 g; Carbo 39.3 g; T Fat 11.8 g; Chol 22.8 mg; Potas 149.0 mg; Sod 83.9 mg.

Cyndie Birken, Texas

BLACK BOTTOMS

1½ cups flour
1 cup sugar
¼ cup baking cocoa
1 teaspoon soda
1 cup water
½ cup oil
1 teaspoon vinegar
1 teaspoon vanilla extract
1 egg
⅓ cup sugar
8 ounces cream cheese, softened
2 cups chocolate chips

Yield: 60 servings

Combine flour, 1 cup sugar, cocoa and soda in bowl; mix well. Add water, oil, vinegar and vanilla; mix well. Cream egg, remaining ⅓ cup sugar and cream cheese in bowl until light and fluffy. Add chocolate chips; mix well. Spoon 1 teaspoon of cocoa mixture in bottom of greased small muffin cups. Top with ½ teaspoon of cream cheese mixture. Bake at 350 degrees for 20 minutes or until light brown.

Approx Per Serving: Cal 89; Prot 1.0 g; Carbo 10.3 g; T Fat 5.4 g; Chol 8.7 mg; Potas 33.0 mg; Sod 27.1 mg.

Helen Stahlman, Maryland

SURPRISE CARROT CAKE

1 2-layer package yellow cake mix
1¼ cups mayonnaise-type salad dressing
4 eggs
2 teaspoons cinnamon
2 cups finely shredded carrots
½ cup chopped walnuts

Yield: 24 servings

Combine cake mix, salad dressing, eggs and cinnamon in bowl; mix well. Stir in carrots and walnuts. Pour into greased 9x13-inch cake pan. Bake at 350 degrees for 35 minutes.

Approx Per Serving: Cal 142; Prot 2.2 g; Carbo 16.3 g; T Fat 7.7 g; Chol 48.8 mg; Potas 54.1 mg; Sod 189.0 mg.

Howard Bennett, Colorado

WHOLE WHEAT CHOCOLATE CAKE

2½ cups whole wheat flour
1 cup sugar
2 teaspoons cinnamon
¼ cup baking cocoa
1 cup water
½ cup oil
1½ teaspoons soda
1 cup buttermilk
2 eggs, beaten
1 teaspoon vanilla extract
2 tablespoons baking cocoa
¼ cup margarine
3 tablespoons low-fat milk
1½ cups confectioners' sugar
¼ cup chopped pecans

Yield: 24 servings

Mix flour, sugar and cinnamon in large mixer bowl. Bring ¼ cup cocoa, water and oil to a boil in saucepan. Pour over flour mixture; mix for 1 minute. Add soda dissolved in buttermilk, eggs and vanilla; mix for 2 minutes. Spoon into greased and floured 10x15-inch baking pan. Bake at 350 degrees for 20 minutes. Bring 2 tablespoons cocoa, butter and milk to a boil in saucepan; remove from heat. Beat in confectioners' sugar and pecans. Spread on warm cake.

Approx Per Serving: Cal 178; Prot 2.9 g; Carbo 24.9 g; T Fat 8.4 g; Chol 23.5 mg; Potas 91.8 mg; Sod 85.9 mg.

Joyce Shepherd, Oklahoma

TEXAS SHEET CAKE

1 cup margarine
1 cup water
¼ cup baking cocoa
2 cups flour
2 cups sugar
½ teaspoon salt
2 eggs
½ cup sour cream
1 teaspoon vanilla extract
1 teaspoon soda
½ cup margarine
¼ cup milk
¼ cup baking cocoa
4 cups confectioners' sugar
1 teaspoon vanilla extract
1 cup chopped nuts

Yield: 48 servings

Bring 1 cup margarine, water and ¼ cup cocoa to a boil in saucepan. Combine flour, sugar and salt in large mixer bowl. Add chocolate mixture; blend well. Add eggs, sour cream, 1 teaspoon vanilla and soda; beat well. Pour into greased 12x18-inch pan. Bake at 350 degrees for 20 minutes. Bring ½ cup margarine, milk and ¼ cup cocoa to a boil in saucepan. Turn off heat. Add confectioners' sugar, vanilla and nuts; mix well. Pour hot frosting over hot cake.

Approx Per Serving: Cal 148; Prot 1.3 g; Carbo 18.1 g; T Fat 8.4 g; Chol 12.7 mg; Potas 36.4 mg; Sod 112.0 mg.

Louella Hanson, New Jersey

Sugarless Fruitcake

1 cup chopped dates
1 cup raisins
1 cup chopped prunes
1/2 cup margarine
2 cups water
2 cups sifted flour
4 eggs, beaten
2 teaspoons soda
2 teaspoons cinnamon
1 teaspoon vanilla extract
1/2 cup chopped pecans

Yield: 24 servings

Bring dates, raisins, prunes, margarine and water to a boil in saucepan. Simmer for 2 minutes; cool. Combine with flour, eggs, soda, cinnamon, vanilla and pecans in bowl; mix well. Spoon into greased and floured 9x13-inch cake pan. Bake at 325 degrees for 40 minutes. Store, well wrapped, in refrigerator or freezer.

Approx Per Serving: Cal 152; Prot 2.8 g;
Carbo 21.9 g; T Fat 6.6 g; Chol 45.7 mg;
Potas 162.0 mg; Sod 126.0 mg.

Lillian Smith, Michigan

Miniature Orange Dip Cupcakes

1/2 cup margarine, softened
1 cup sugar
2 eggs
2 cups flour
1 teaspoon soda
2/3 cup buttermilk
1 cup chopped dates
1/2 cup chopped walnuts
1 tablespoon grated orange rind
1 cup orange juice concentrate
1 cup sugar
1 tablespoon grated orange rind

Yield: 24 cupcakes

Cream margarine and 1 cup sugar in mixer bowl until light and fluffy. Beat in eggs. Add flour and soda alternately with buttermilk, mixing well after each addition. Stir in dates, walnuts and 1 tablespoon orange rind. Spoon into greased miniature muffin cups. Bake at 350 degrees for 15 minutes. Heat orange juice, 1 cup sugar and 1 tablespoon orange rind in saucepan. Dip cupcakes into hot mixture. Cool on wire rack.

Approx Per Cupcake: Cal 166; Prot 2.4 g;
Carbo 31.9 g; T Fat 6.0 g; Chol 23.1 mg;
Potas 109.0 mg; Sod 93.0 mg.

Nora Edwards, Ohio

Peach Dessert Cake

1/2 cup margarine, softened
1/2 cup sugar
2 eggs
3/4 cup plus 2 tablespoons flour
1 teaspoon baking powder
1/4 teaspoon salt
3 cups sliced peaches
1/3 cup sugar
1/2 teaspoon cinnamon

Yield: 12 servings

Cream margarine, 1/2 cup sugar and eggs in mixer bowl until light and fluffy. Combine flour, baking powder and salt. Add to creamed mixture gradually; mix well. Spread in 9x13-inch pan. Arrange peaches over top of batter. Sprinkle with mixture of remaining 1/3 cup sugar and cinnamon. Bake at 325 degrees for 45 minutes.

Approx Per Serving: Cal 186; Prot 2.3 g;
Carbo 25.6 g; T Fat 8.7 g; Chol 45.4 mg;
Potas 107.0 mg; Sod 149.0 mg.

Frank Hamilton, North Carolina

POPPY SEED CAKE

1 2-layer package lemon cake
   mix
1 4-ounce package vanilla
   instant pudding mix
   3/4 cup oil
   3/4 cup water
   4 eggs
1 1-ounce jar poppy seed

Yield: 24 servings

Combine cake mix, pudding mix, oil, water and eggs in bowl; mix well. Add poppy seed; mix well. Pour into greased bundt pan. Bake at 350 degrees for 45 to 50 minutes or until cake tests done. Invert onto wire rack to cool.

Approx Per Serving: Cal 147; Prot 1.6 g;
Carbo 15.3 g; T Fat 8.9 g; Chol 45.6 mg;
Potas 11.2 mg; Sod 122.5 mg.

Esther Jackson, Georgia

PUMPKIN CAKE

1 1/2 cups flour
1 tablespoon baking powder
1 teaspoon cinnamon
1/4 teaspoon cloves
1/4 teaspoon nutmeg
1/4 cup dried currants
4 egg yolks
2 tablespoons plus 2 teaspoons
   light brown sugar
2 tablespoons plus 2 teaspoons
   oil
3/4 cup canned pumpkin
1/4 cup unsweetened orange
   juice
1 teaspoon grated orange rind
1 teaspoon vanilla extract
4 egg whites
1/8 teaspoon salt
2 tablespoons confectioners'
   sugar
1/2 teaspoon hot water
1/4 teaspoon grated orange rind

Yield: 8 servings

Sift flour, baking powder and spices together. Toss currants with 2 teaspoons flour mixture in small bowl until well coated; set aside. Combine egg yolks, brown sugar and oil in mixer bowl; beat for 3 minutes or until thickened. Stir in pumpkin, orange juice, 1 teaspoon orange rind and vanilla. Add sifted dry ingredients; mix well. Stir in currants. Beat egg whites with salt in mixer bowl until stiff peaks form. Stir 1/4 of the egg whites gently into batter. Fold in remaining egg whites gently. Spoon into 6-cup fluted cake pan sprayed with nonstick cooking spray. Bake at 350 degrees on center rack of oven for 1 1/4 hours or until tester inserted in center comes out clean. Invert onto wire rack to cool. Blend confectioners' sugar with water in bowl. Stir in 1/4 teaspoon orange rind. Drizzle over cake.

Approx Per Serving: Cal 212; Prot 6.0 g;
Carbo 29.9 g; T Fat 7.6 g; Chol 137.0 mg;
Potas 174.0 mg; Sod 197.0 mg.

Sue Roller, Florida

COUNTRY SPICE CAKE

3 cups flour
2 cups packed brown sugar
1½ teaspoons baking powder
¾ teaspoon soda
1 tablespoon cinnamon
½ teaspoon nutmeg
⅛ teaspoon ginger
½ teaspoon salt
1½ cups plain yogurt
¾ cup margarine, softened
3 eggs
½ teaspoon vanilla extract

Yield: 16 servings

Mix first 8 ingredients in mixer bowl. Add yogurt, margarine, eggs and vanilla; mix at low speed until ingredients are moistened, scraping bowl frequently. Beat on high speed for 2 minutes. Spoon into greased and floured 9-inch bundt pan. Bake at 350 degrees for 55 minutes to 1 hour or until toothpick inserted in center comes out clean. Cool in pan for 10 minutes. Invert onto wire rack to cool completely.

Approx Per Serving: Cal 293; Prot 4.8 g; Carbo 46.0 g; T Fat 10.1 g; Chol 52.7 mg; Potas 183.0 mg; Sod 246.0 mg.

Kimberly Adams, Iowa

STATE FAIR SPONGE CAKE

1¼ cups cake flour
1 cup sugar
½ teaspoon baking powder
6 egg whites
1 teaspoon cream of tartar
½ cup sugar
6 egg yolks
¼ cup water
1 teaspoon vanilla extract

Yield: 16 servings

Sift first 3 ingredients together. Beat egg whites with cream of tartar until foamy. Beat in remaining ½ cup sugar gradually until stiff peaks form. Combine egg yolks, water, vanilla and sifted ingredients in mixer bowl. Beat at medium speed for 4 minutes. Fold into egg whites. Pour into 10-inch tube pan. Bake at 350 degrees for 45 minutes. Invert to cool.

Approx Per Serving: Cal 133; Prot 2.9 g; Carbo 25.7 g; T Fat 2.2 g; Chol 103.0 mg; Potas 40.8 mg; Sod 36.4 mg.

Kelly Adkins, Pennsylvania

EGGLESS TEA CAKE

½ cup shortening
1 cup sugar
2 cups sifted flour
1 teaspoon baking powder
½ teaspoon soda
¼ teaspoon salt
1 teaspoon each cinnamon,
allspice and nutmeg
1 cup milk

Yield: 10 servings

Cream shortening and sugar in mixer bowl until light and fluffy. Add mixture of sifted flour, baking powder, soda, salt and spices alternately with milk, mixing well after each addition. Spoon into greased cake pan. Bake at 375 degrees for 45 to 50 minutes or until cake tests done.

Approx Per Serving: Cal 274; Prot 3.4 g; Carbo 40.2 g; T Fat 11.3 g; Chol 3.3 mg; Potas 57.7 mg; Sod 138.0 mg.

Kate Runyon, Louisiana

BANANA COOKIES

1 1/2 cups sifted flour
1 cup sugar
1/2 teaspoon soda
1/4 teaspoon nutmeg
3/4 teaspoon cinnamon
3/4 cup shortening
1 egg, well beaten
1 cup mashed bananas
1 teaspoon vanilla extract
1 3/4 cups oats
1/2 cup chopped walnuts

Yield: 42 cookies

Sift flour, sugar, soda, nutmeg and cinnamon into bowl. Cut in shortening until crumbly. Add egg, bananas, vanilla, oats and walnuts; mix well. Drop by teaspoonfuls 1 1/2 inches apart onto ungreased cookie sheets. Bake at 350 degrees for 10 minutes or until edges are brown. Remove immediately to wire rack to cool.

Approx Per Cookie: Cal 95; Prot 1.4 g; Carbo 11.7 g; T Fat 5.0 g; Chol 6.5 mg; Potas 45.8 mg; Sod 11.7 mg.

Amanda Murray, Iowa

BLUEBERRY BARS

2 1/2 cups flour
1/2 cup sugar
1 egg, slightly beaten
1/2 teaspoon baking powder
1 cup margarine, softened
2 cups fresh blueberries
1/4 cup sugar
1 tablespoon lemon juice
1 tablespoon grated lemon rind
2 tablespoons cornstarch

Yield: 48 bars

Combine flour, 1/2 cup sugar, egg and baking powder in bowl; mix well. Cut in margarine until crumbly. Reserve 1/2 cup mixture. Press remaining dough into ball. Roll on floured surface. Press over bottom and up sides of 10x15-inch baking dish. Dough will be crumbly. Pieces can be pressed together in pan. Combine blueberries, 1/4 cup sugar, lemon juice, lemon rind and cornstarch in bowl; mix well. Pour into prepared dish. Roll out reserved dough. Cut into strips. Arrange lattice-fashion over top of blueberries. Sprinkle with additional sugar. Bake at 375 degrees for 25 to 30 minutes. Cool. Cut into bars.

Approx Per Bar: Cal 76; Prot 0.9 g; Carbo 9.3 g; T Fat 4.0 g; Chol 6.1 mg; Potas 14.9 mg; Sod 37.9 mg.

Eleanor Irvin, Texas

BROWNIES

1 cup margarine
3 tablespoons baking cocoa
1 cup water
2 cups sugar
2 cups flour
2 eggs
1/2 cup buttermilk
1 teaspoon soda
1 teaspoon vanilla extract
1 1/3 cups sugar
6 tablespoons margarine
6 tablespoons milk
1/2 cup semisweet chocolate chips
1/2 teaspoon vanilla extract

Yield: 72 brownies

Melt 1 cup margarine in saucepan. Add cocoa and water; mix well. Bring to a boil. Remove from heat; cool. Sift 2 cups sugar and flour into bowl. Stir in cocoa mixture. Add eggs, buttermilk, soda and 1 teaspoon vanilla; mix well. Pour into greased 10x15-inch baking pan. Bake at 375 degrees for 20 minutes. Reduce temperature to 350 degrees. Bake until brownies test done. Combine 1 1/3 cups sugar, 6 tablespoons margarine and milk in saucepan. Bring to a boil. Cook for 1 minute, stirring constantly. Remove from heat. Add chocolate chips and 1/2 teaspoon vanilla. Beat until smooth and creamy. Spread over brownies.

Approx Per Brownie: Cal 89; Prot 0.8 g; Carbo 12.8 g; T Fat 4.2 g; Chol 7.9 mg; Potas 18.3 mg; Sod 57.0 mg.

Margie Weston, Oklahoma

CARROT COOKIES

3/4 cup margarine, softened
1 cup sugar
1 egg, beaten
1 cup mashed cooked carrots
2 cups flour
2 teaspoons baking powder
1/4 teaspoon salt
2 cups confectioners' sugar
1 tablespoon melted margarine
1/2 teaspoon lemon juice
Grated rind of 1 orange
Juice from 1 orange

Yield: 36 cookies

Cream 3/4 cup margarine and sugar in bowl until light and fluffy. Add egg; beat well. Add carrots alternately with mixture of flour, baking powder and salt; mix well. Drop by teaspoonfuls onto cookie sheet. Bake at 350 degrees for 10 to 12 minutes or until brown. Cool on wire rack. Combine confectioners' sugar, 1 tablespoon melted margarine, lemon juice, orange rind and orange juice in bowl; mix until of spreading consistency. Spread on cookies.

Approx Per Cookie: Cal 116; Prot 1.0 g; Carbo 18.6 g; T Fat 4.4 g; Chol 7.6 mg; Potas 29.9 mg; Sod 73.1 mg.

Jill Winter, Colorado

CHOCOLATE CHIP COOKIES

1 cup margarine, softened
3/4 cup sugar
3/4 cup packed brown sugar
1 teaspoon vanilla extract
2 eggs
2¼ cups flour
1 teaspoon soda
2 cups semisweet chocolate chips

Yield: 60 cookies

Cream margarine, sugar, brown sugar and vanilla in bowl until light and fluffy. Add eggs; mix until smooth. Stir in mixture of flour and soda. Add chocolate chips; mix well. Drop by teaspoonfuls onto greased cookie sheets. Bake at 370 degrees for 8 to 10 minutes or until golden brown.

Approx Per Cookie: Cal 95; Prot 1.0 g; Carbo 12.0 g; T Fat 5.3 g; Chol 9.1 mg; Potas 36.9 mg; Sod 44.0 mg.

Melanie Jacobs, Nebraska

COCOA MERINGUES

3 egg whites, at room temperature
1 teaspoon vanilla extract
1/8 teaspoon salt
1/8 teaspoon cream of tartar
1 cup sugar
3 tablespoons baking cocoa

Yield: 36 meringues

Combine egg whites, vanilla, salt and cream of tartar in bowl. Beat until soft peaks form. Add sugar gradually, beating constantly until stiff peaks form. Fold in cocoa gently; do not beat. Drop by heaping tablespoonfuls onto foil-lined cookie sheets. Bake at 250 degrees for 1 hour. Let stand for 5 minutes. Remove from foil.

Approx Per Meringue: Cal 24; Prot 0.4 g; Carbo 5.8 g; T Fat 0.1 g; Chol 0.0 mg; Potas 9.6 mg; Sod 12.1 mg.

Mindy Thaler, Iowa

COCONUT MACAROONS

2 cups flaked coconut
1/2 cup sweetened condensed milk
1 teaspoon vanilla extract

Yield: 24 cookies

Combine coconut and condensed milk in bowl. Add vanilla; mix well. Drop by teaspoonfuls 1 inch apart onto greased cookie sheet. Bake at 350 degrees for 10 minutes or until light brown. Remove to wire rack immediately.

Approx Per Cookie: Cal 44; Prot 0.7 g; Carbo 4.5 g; T Fat 2.8 g; Chol 2.2 mg; Potas 47.4 mg; Sod 9.4 mg.

Constance Spahn, Vermont

Cookie Crunch

1 cup margarine, softened
1 cup sugar
1 egg yolk
2 cups flour
1 teaspoon cinnamon
1 egg white
1/3 cup chopped pecans

Yield: 40 servings

Cream margarine with fork in bowl. Blend in sugar and egg yolk. Add sifted flour and cinnamon; mix well. Press onto ungreased 10x15-inch baking sheet. Brush with unbeaten egg white. Sprinkle with pecans. Bake at 350 degrees for 25 minutes. Cut into squares while hot.

Approx Per Serving: Cal 91; Prot 0.9 g; Carbo 10.0 g; T Fat 5.4 g; Chol 6.8 mg; Potas 14.1 mg; Sod 55.0 mg.

Luellen Resnik, Utah

Country Morning Cookies

1 1/2 cups packed brown sugar
1 1/2 cups margarine, softened
2 eggs, beaten
1 1/2 teaspoons vanilla extract
2 1/2 cups flour
3/4 teaspoon soda
1   16-ounce package oat cereal with raisins and dates
3/4 cup raisins
3/4 cup chopped dates

Yield: 84 cookies

Beat brown sugar and margarine in mixer bowl until light and fluffy. Add eggs and vanilla; mix well. Add mixture of flour and soda; mix well. Stir in cereal, raisins and dates. Drop by level measuring tablespoonfuls onto cookie sheet. Bake at 350 degrees for 12 minutes or until brown. Cool slightly on cookie sheet. Remove to wire rack to cool completely.

Approx Per Cookie: Cal 92; Prot 1.2 g; Carbo 12.6 g; T Fat 4.4 g; Chol 6.5 mg; Potas 68.2 mg; Sod 51.5 mg.

Ruby Brown, Virginia

Cream Cheese Cookies

1 cup margarine, softened
3 ounces cream cheese, softened
1 cup sugar
1 egg yolk
2 tablespoons vanilla extract
2 1/2 cups sifted flour

Yield: 36 cookies

Combine margarine, cream cheese, sugar, egg yolk and vanilla in mixer bowl. Beat until light and fluffy. Add flour gradually, beating until well mixed. Chill dough until firm enough to handle. Shape into 1-inch balls. Place 2 inches apart on cookie sheet. Press center of each with thumb to flatten. Bake at 325 degrees for 25 minutes or until golden brown on bottom. May place a small amount of preserves in indentation. May substitute almond extract for vanilla.

Approx Per Cookie: Cal 106; Prot 1.2 g; Carbo 11.7 g; T Fat 6.2 g; Chol 10.2 mg; Potas 12.6 mg; Sod 50.5 mg.

Kathy Carlson, Idaho

Forgotten Cookies

2 egg whites
1/4 teaspoon salt
2/3 cup sugar
4 drops of vanilla extract
1 cup chopped pecans
1 cup chocolate chips

Yield: 36 cookies

Combine egg whites and salt in mixer bowl; beat until stiff peaks form. Mix in sugar gradually. Stir in vanilla and pecans. Fold in chocolate chips gently. Drop by heaping teaspoonfuls onto foil-lined cookie sheet. Place cookies in preheated 350-degree oven; turn off oven. Let stand for 2 hours to overnight.

Approx Per Cookie: Cal 61; Prot 0.6 g; Carbo 7.0 g; T Fat 3.9 g; Chol 0.0 mg; Potas 32.0 mg; Sod 18.4 mg.

Joan Shoemaker, Kansas

Gingersnaps

3/4 cup shortening
1 cup packed brown sugar
1/4 cup molasses
1 egg
2 1/4 cups flour
2 teaspoons soda
1 teaspoon ginger
1 teaspoon cinnamon
1/2 teaspoon cloves
1/4 cup sugar

Yield: 60 cookies

Cream shortening, brown sugar, molasses and egg in bowl until light and fluffy. Add sifted mixture of flour, soda, ginger, cinnamon and cloves; mix well. Shape into 1-inch balls. Roll in sugar. Place 2 inches apart on greased cookie sheets. Bake at 375 degrees for 8 to 10 minutes. Cool slightly. Remove to wire rack to cool.

Approx Per Cookie: Cal 61; Prot 0.6 g; Carbo 8.7 g; T Fat 2.7 g; Chol 4.6 mg; Potas 57.2 mg; Sod 31.5 mg.

Miriam Strong, Minnesota

Healthy Bars

1/3 cup packed brown sugar
1/3 cup oil
1/4 cup apple juice concentrate
1 cup whole wheat flour
1/2 cup oat bran cereal
1 1/2 cups oats
1 cup chopped dates
1 cup raisins

Yield: 24 bars

Combine brown sugar, oil and apple juice concentrate in bowl; mix well. Mix flour, cereal and oats in large bowl. Stir in dates and raisins. Add sugar mixture, stirring until crumbly. Spoon into 9-inch baking dish sprayed with nonstick cooking spray. Bake at 375 degrees for 20 minutes or until cake tests done. Cool. Cut into bars.

Approx Per Bar: Cal 120; Prot 2.2 g; Carbo 22.4 g; T Fat 3.5 g; Chol 0.0 mg; Potas 160.0 mg; Sod 3.2 mg.

Michelle Petain, Louisiana

MAPLE SYRUP COOKIES

1 egg, beaten
1/2 cup margarine, softened
1/2 teaspoon vanilla extract
1/2 cup maple syrup
2 cups flour
1/2 teaspoon soda
1/2 cup chopped pecans
1 cup confectioners' sugar
2 tablespoons margarine, softened
1/4 cup maple syrup

Yield: 36 cookies

Combine first 4 ingredients in mixer bowl; beat well. Stir in flour and soda; mix well. Stir in pecans. Drop by teaspoonfuls onto greased cookie sheet. Flatten with fork. Bake at 350 degrees for 10 minutes or until brown. Cool on wire rack. Combine confectioners' sugar, 2 tablespoons margarine and enough remaining 1/4 cup maple syrup to make of spreading consistency. Spread over cookies.

Approx Per Cookie: Cal 94; Prot 1.1 g; Carbo 12.6 g; T Fat 4.5 g; Chol 7.6 mg; Potas 25.2 mg; Sod 49.7 mg.

Theresa Jackson, Vermont

TWICE-BAKED COOKIES

1 cup sugar
1/2 cup oil
4 eggs
1/2 teaspoon grated lemon rind
1 teaspoon vanilla extract
3 1/2 cups flour
2 teaspoons baking powder
1/8 teaspoon salt
2 tablespoons sugar
1/8 teaspoon cinnamon

Yield: 48 cookies

Beat 1 cup sugar and oil until smooth. Beat in eggs 1 at a time. Mix in lemon rind and vanilla. Add flour, baking powder and salt; mix well. Shape into small loaves on greased cookie sheet. Sprinkle with 2 tablespoons sugar and cinnamon. Bake at 350 degrees for 30 to 40 minutes. Turn off oven. Slice loaves into cookies. Place on cookie sheet. Place in warm oven until crisp.

Approx Per Cookie: Cal 78; Prot 1.5 g; Carbo 11.7 g; T Fat 2.8 g; Chol 22.8 mg; Potas 14.6 mg; Sod 25.5 mg.

Darlene Rosenberg, Illinois

MUD BAR COOKIES

1/2 cup margarine, softened
3/4 cup packed brown sugar
1 teaspoon vanilla extract
1 egg
1 cup plus 2 tablespoons flour
1/2 teaspoon soda
1/2 teaspoon salt
1/2 cup chopped pecans
2 cups semisweet chocolate chips

Yield: 36 bars

Cream first 3 ingredients in mixer bowl until light and fluffy. Add egg; mix well. Add mixture of flour, soda and salt; mix well. Stir in pecans and 1 1/2 cups chocolate chips. Spoon into foil-lined 9x13-inch baking pan. Bake at 375 degrees for 23 to 25 minutes or until edges pull away from sides of pan. Sprinkle with 1/2 cup chocolate chips while hot. Spread over top when melted.

Approx Per Bar: Cal 113; Prot 1.1 g; Carbo 12.8 g; T Fat 7.3 g; Chol 7.6 mg; Potas 61.2 mg; Sod 67.9 mg.

Harriet Carroon, Tennessee

No-Bake Cookies

1/2 cup margarine
2 cups sugar
1/4 cup baking cocoa
1/2 cup milk
2 teaspoons vanilla extract
2 1/2 cups quick-cooking oats
1/2 cup peanut butter

Yield: 54 cookies

Melt margarine in saucepan. Add sugar, cocoa and milk. Bring to a boil. Cook over medium heat for 2 minutes, stirring constantly. Remove from heat. Add vanilla, oats and peanut butter; mix well. Drop by teaspoonfuls onto waxed paper. Cool. Store in airtight container.

Approx Per Cookie: Cal 75; Prot 1.4 g; Carbo 10.6 g; T Fat 3.3 g; Chol 0.3 mg; Potas 38.0 mg; Sod 25.3 mg.

Lee Anne Houston, Texas

Chocolate Chip-Oatmeal Cookies

1 cup margarine, softened
3/4 cup sugar
3/4 cup packed brown sugar
2 eggs
1 teaspoon vanilla extract
1 3/4 cups flour
1 teaspoon soda
2 cups oats
1 cup semisweet chocolate chips
1 cup chopped walnuts

Yield: 72 cookies

Cream margarine, sugar and brown sugar in bowl until light and fluffy. Add eggs and vanilla; mix well. Stir in flour, soda, oats, chocolate chips and walnuts. Drop by teaspoonfuls onto greased cookie sheets. Bake at 350 degrees for 12 to 15 minutes or until brown. Cool on wire rack.

Approx Per Cookie: Cal 84; Prot 1.2 g; Carbo 9.8 g; T Fat 4.7 g; Chol 7.6 mg; Potas 38.5 mg; Sod 44.7 mg.

Jean Biggerman, Tennessee

"M&M's" Cookies

1 cup margarine, softened
1 cup sugar
1/2 cup packed brown sugar
2 eggs
2 teaspoons vanilla extract
2 1/4 cups flour
1 teaspoon soda
1/2 teaspoon salt
12 ounces "M&M's" Plain Chocolate candies

Yield: 84 cookies

Cream margarine, sugar and brown sugar in mixer bowl until light and fluffy. Beat in eggs and vanilla. Add mixture of flour, soda and salt; mix well. Stir in candies. Drop by teaspoonfuls onto ungreased cookie sheet. Bake at 375 degrees for 8 to 10 minutes or until light brown.

Approx Per Cookie: Cal 68; Prot 0.8 g; Carbo 8.5 g; T Fat 3.6 g; Chol 7.4 mg; Potas 23.7 mg; Sod 46.5 mg.

Carolyn Dickinson, California

Double Chocolate Oatmeal Cookies

1/2 cup sugar
1 cup margarine, softened
1 egg
1/4 cup water
1 teaspoon vanilla extract
1 1/4 cups flour
3 cups quick-cooking oats
1/3 cup baking cocoa
1/2 teaspoon soda
1 cup chocolate chips

Yield: 66 cookies

Combine sugar, margarine, egg, water and vanilla in mixer bowl; mix until smooth. Stir in flour, oats, cocoa, soda and chocolate chips. Drop by rounded teaspoonfuls 2 inches apart onto ungreased cookie sheet. Bake at 350 degrees for 10 minutes or until light brown. Remove to wire rack to cool.

Approx Per Cookie: Cal 69; Prot 1.1 g; Carbo 7.5 g; T Fat 4.1 g; Chol 4.2 mg; Potas 31.6 mg; Sod 40.3 mg.

Ruth Winston, South Carolina

Orange Drop Cookies

3/4 cup shortening
1 1/4 cups sugar
2 eggs
3 cups flour
1 tablespoon baking powder
2/3 cup orange juice
2 teaspoons grated orange rind

Yield: 48 cookies

Cream shortening, sugar and eggs in large bowl until light and fluffy. Add flour and baking powder; mix well. Stir in orange juice and orange rind. Drop by teaspoonfuls onto cookie sheets. Bake at 350 degrees for 10 to 15 minutes or until lightly browned.

Approx Per Cookie: Cal 82; Prot 1.1 g; Carbo 11.6 g; T Fat 3.5 g; Chol 11.4 mg; Potas 17.6 mg; Sod 24.1 mg.

Edna Ellington, Oklahoma

Peanut Butter Squares

2 cups peanut butter
1/2 cup melted margarine
1/2 cup packed brown sugar
1/2 teaspoon vanilla extract
2 1/2 cups confectioners' sugar
1 1/2 cups semisweet chocolate chips
2 tablespoons margarine

Yield: 100 squares

Combine peanut butter, 1/2 cup melted margarine, brown sugar, vanilla and confectioners' sugar in bowl; mix well. Press into 9x13-inch baking dish. Melt chocolate chips and 2 tablespoons margarine in saucepan, stirring frequently. Spread over peanut butter layer. Chill in refrigerator until set. Cut into squares.

Approx Per Square: Cal 67; Prot 1.6 g; Carbo 5.8 g; T Fat 4.7 g; Chol 0.0 mg; Potas 48.5 mg; Sod 31.4 mg.

Holly Winters, Texas

PEANUT BUTTER COOKIES

½ cup margarine, softened
½ cup peanut butter
½ cup sugar
½ cup packed brown sugar
1 egg, beaten
½ teaspoon vanilla extract
½ teaspoon soda
2 cups flour

Yield: 50 cookies

Cream margarine, peanut butter, sugar and brown sugar in mixer bowl until light and fluffy. Add egg, vanilla and mixture of soda and flour; mix well. Shape into walnut-sized balls. Place on cookie sheet; flatten with fork. May refrigerate before shaping into balls to stiffen dough. Bake at 350 degrees for 10 minutes or until firm. Cool on wire rack.

Approx Per Cookie: Cal 67; Prot 1.4 g; Carbo 8.3 g; T Fat 3.3 g; Chol 5.4 mg; Potas 32.0 mg; Sod 21.4 mg.

Barbara Walter, Mississippi

PINEAPPLE COOKIES

¼ cup margarine, softened
½ cup sugar
½ cup packed brown sugar
1 egg, beaten
1   20-ounce can juice-pack crushed pineapple, drained
1¼ cups flour
½ cups oats
½ teaspoon soda
½ teaspoon salt
½ teaspoon cinnamon
½ teaspoon nutmeg

Yield: 36 cookies

Cream margarine, sugar and brown sugar in large mixer bowl until light and fluffy. Add egg and pineapple; mix well. Mix flour, oats, soda, salt, cinnamon and nutmeg in bowl. Add to margarine mixture; mix well. Drop by teaspoonfuls onto cookie sheet. Bake at 375 degrees for 12 minutes or until brown. Cool on wire rack.

Approx Per Cookie: Cal 74; Prot 1.3 g; Carbo 13.8 g; T Fat 1.7 g; Chol 7.7 mg; Potas 48.3 mg; Sod 55.5 mg.

Teresa Allison, Nevada

PUDDING COOKIES

⅔ cup flour
½ teaspoon soda
½ teaspoon cream of tartar
¼ teaspoon salt
1   4-ounce package pudding mix
½ cup shortening
1 egg
½ teaspoon vanilla extract
1 cup oats

Yield: 30 cookies

Combine flour, soda, cream of tartar and salt in mixer bowl. Add pudding mix, shortening, egg and vanilla. Beat for 2 minutes or until smooth. Stir in oats. Drop by teaspoonfuls onto greased cookie sheet. Flatten with fork dipped in cold water. Bake at 375 degrees for 8 minutes; do not overbake. May add chocolate chips or chopped pecans or walnuts.

Approx Per Cookie: Cal 67; Prot 0.9 g; Carbo 7.5 g; T Fat 3.8 g; Chol 9.1 mg; Potas 16.4 mg; Sod 59.2 mg.

Margaret Jorgenson, New York

HONEY OATMEAL COOKIES

1 cup margarine, softened
1 cup packed brown sugar
2 eggs
1/2 cup honey
1 teaspoon vanilla extract
3 1/2 cups sifted flour
2 teaspoons soda
2 cups quick-cooking oats
1/2 cup coconut

Yield: 72 cookies

Cream margarine and brown sugar in large bowl until light and fluffy. Beat in eggs; mix well. Beat in honey and vanilla. Combine flour, soda, oats and coconut. Add to creamed mixture; mix well. Drop by teaspoonfuls onto ungreased cookie sheet. Bake at 350 degrees for 12 to 14 minutes or until lightly browned.

Approx Per Cookie: Cal 76; Prot 1.2 g; Carbo 11.0 g; T Fat 3.1 g; Chol 7.6 mg; Potas 30.2 mg; Sod 57.8 mg.

Belle Diefenbach, Maryland

O'HENRY BARS

1 cup sugar
1 cup light corn syrup
1 1/4 cups chunky peanut butter
6 cups Special-K cereal
2 cups chocolate chips

Yield: 36 bars

Combine sugar and syrup in large saucepan. Bring to a boil. Remove from heat. Stir in peanut butter and cereal. Press evenly onto greased 9x13-inch baking dish. Melt chocolate chips in double boiler. Spread over cereal layer. Cool. Cut into bars.

Approx Per Bar: Cal 114; Prot 3.3 g; Carbo 16.4 g; T Fat 4.6 g; Chol 0.0 mg; Potas 69.2 mg; Sod 73.5 mg.

Sylvia Bennington, Kansas

REFRIGERATOR COOKIES

3/4 cup margarine, softened
1 cup sugar
2 tablespoons milk
2 eggs, beaten
1/2 teaspoon salt
1 teaspoon vanilla extract
2 teaspoons nutmeg
2 cups flour
2 teaspoons baking powder

Yield: 36 cookies

Cream margarine and sugar in mixer bowl until light and fluffy. Add milk, eggs, salt, vanilla and nutmeg; mix well. Stir in sifted flour and baking powder gradually. Chill in refrigerator. Roll 1/8 inch thick on floured surface. Cut as desired. Place on cookie sheet. Bake at 350 degrees for 12 minutes or until edges are light brown. Sprinkle with additional sugar if desired. Remove to wire rack to cool.

Approx Per Cookie: Cal 86; Prot 1.1 g; Carbo 11.0 g; T Fat 4.3 g; Chol 15.7 mg; Potas 13.5 mg; Sod 84.6 mg.

Arlene Atchison, California

Swedish Apple Pie

1 egg
1/3 cup sugar
1/3 cup packed brown sugar
1/2 cup flour
1 teaspoon baking powder
1 teaspoon cinnamon
2 cups chopped peeled apples
1 teaspoon vanilla extract
1/2 cup chopped pecans
Cinnamon-sugar

Yield: 8 servings

Combine egg, sugar, brown sugar, flour, baking powder, cinnamon, apples, vanilla and pecans in bowl, mixing well after each addition. Pour into greased 8-inch pie plate. Sprinkle with cinnamon-sugar. Bake at 350 degrees for 30 to 35 minutes or until apples are tender and the topping is brown.

Approx Per Serving: Cal 151; Prot 1.8 g;
Carbo 25.9 g; T Fat 5.3 g; Chol 30.5 mg;
Potas 96.0 mg; Sod 48.2 mg.

Alice Weaver, Idaho

Coconut Pies

4 eggs, beaten
1 3/4 cups sugar
1/2 cup buttermilk baking mix
1/4 cup melted margarine
1 teaspoon vanilla extract
2 cups milk
1 7-ounce can coconut

Yield: 12 servings

Beat eggs and sugar in bowl until light and fluffy. Add baking mix, margarine, vanilla and milk; mix well. Stir in coconut. Pour into two 9-inch pie plates. Bake at 325 degrees until brown. This pie makes it own crust.

Approx Per Serving: Cal 276; Prot 4.1 g;
Carbo 38.8 g; T Fat 12.5 g; Chol 97.0 mg;
Potas 134.0 mg; Sod 92.7 mg.

Montie Hart, Oklahoma

Pink Rhubarb Pie

2 cups chopped rhubarb
2 teaspoons artificial sweetener
2 tablespoons water
1 3-ounce package sugar-free strawberry gelatin
10 packets aspertame artificial sweetener
1 tablespoon lemon juice
2 cups whipped topping
1 baked 9-inch pie shell

Yield: 8 servings

Combine rhubarb, artificial sweetener and water in saucepan. Cook over low heat until rhubarb is tender. Remove from heat. Stir in gelatin and aspertame until dissolved. Cool slightly. Add lemon juice; mix well. Cool to room temperature. Fold in whipped topping. Pour into pie shell. Chill until firm.

Approx Per Serving: Cal 182; Prot 2.3 g;
Carbo 15.7 g; T Fat 12.3 g; Chol 0.0 mg;
Potas 104.0 mg; Sod 175.0 mg.

Peggy Bynum, North Dakota

SOUTHERN STRAWBERRY PIE

3/4 cup sugar
2 tablespoons cornstarch
2 tablespoons light corn syrup
1 cup water
3 tablespoons strawberry
gelatin
1 quart whole strawberries
1 baked 9-inch pie shell

Yield: 6 servings

Combine sugar, cornstarch, corn syrup and water in saucepan. Bring to a boil. Cook until clear and thickened, stirring constantly. Stir in gelatin until dissolved; cool. Arrange strawberries in pie shell. Pour gelatin mixture over berries. Chill until firm.

Approx Per Serving: Cal 251; Prot 2.3 g;
Carbo 44.0 g; T Fat 7.3 g; Chol 0.0 mg;
Potas 139.0 mg; Sod 161.0 mg.

Sue Scott, New Mexico

SURPRISE WATERMELON PIE

1 cup buttermilk baking mix
3 tablespoons boiling water
1/4 cup margarine
1/2 cup sugar
1   3-ounce package sugar-free
mixed fruit gelatin
3 tablespoons cornstarch
11/2 cups water
3 cups watermelon ball halves

Yield: 6 servings

Mix baking mix, boiling water and margarine in pie plate until crumbly. Press over bottom and side of pie plate. Bake at 450 degrees for 10 minutes. Cool. Combine sugar, gelatin, cornstarch and water in saucepan. Cook until thickened, stirring constantly. Cool. Add watermelon. Spoon into cooled pie shell. Chill until serving time. Garnish with whipped topping.

Approx Per Serving: Cal 222; Prot 3.4 g;
Carbo 39.9 g; T Fat 11.0 g; Chol 0.0 mg;
Potas 128.0 mg; Sod 401.0 mg.

Wilma Flint, Michigan

LOW-CHOLESTEROL PIE PASTRY

2 cups flour
1 teaspoon low-sodium salt
1/4 cup oil
3 tablespoons cold low-fat milk

Yield: 2 pie shells

Sift flour and salt into bowl. Add mixture of oil and milk; stir gently until mixture clings together. Divide dough into 2 portions. Chill, covered, for several minutes. Roll into 9-inch circles between waxed paper. Line pie plate with 1 circle. Fill with desired filling. Cover with remaining pastry. Seal edges; flute and cut vents. Bake until brown.

Approx Per Shell: Cal 707; Prot 13.8 g;
Carbo 96.0 g; T Fat 28.9 g; Chol 2.0 mg;
Potas 621.5 mg; Sod 13.6 mg.

Rita Stone, Wisconsin

NO-SALT SEASONING

Salt is an acquired taste and can be significantly reduced in the diet by learning to use herbs and spices instead. When using fresh herbs, use 3 times the amount of dried herbs. Begin with small amounts to determine your favorite tastes. A dash of fresh lemon or lime juice can also wake up your taste buds.

Herb Blends to Replace Salt

Combine all ingredients in small airtight container. Add several grains of rice to prevent caking.

No-Salt Surprise Seasoning — 2 teaspoons garlic powder and 1 teaspoon each of dried basil, oregano and dehydrated lemon juice.

Pungent Salt Substitute — 3 teaspoons dried basil, 2 teaspoons each of summer savory, celery seed, cumin seed, sage and marjoram, and 1 teaspoon lemon thyme; crush with mortar and pestle.

Spicy No-Salt Seasoning — 1 teaspoon each cloves, pepper and coriander, 2 teaspoons paprika and 1 tablespoon dried rosemary; crush with mortar and pestle.

Herb Complements

Beef — bay leaf, chives, cumin, garlic, hot pepper, marjoram, rosemary

Pork — coriander, cumin, garlic, ginger, hot pepper, savory, thyme

Poultry — garlic, oregano, rosemary, savory, sage

Cheese — basil, chives, curry, dill, marjoram, oregano, parsley, sage, thyme

Fish — chives, coriander, dill, garlic, tarragon, thyme

Fruit — cinnamon, coriander, cloves, ginger, mint

Bread —caraway, marjoram, oregano, poppy seed, rosemary, thyme

Salads — basil, chives, tarragon, parsley, sorrel

Vegetables — basil, chives, dill, tarragon, marjoram, mint, parsley, pepper

Basic Herb Butter

Combine 1 stick unsalted butter, 1 to 3 tablespoons dried herbs or twice that amount of minced fresh herbs of choice, 1/2 teaspoon lemon juice and white pepper to taste. Let stand for 1 hour or longer before using.

Basic Herb Vinegar

Heat vinegar of choice in saucepan; do not boil. Pour into bottle; add 1 or more herbs of choice and seal bottle. Let stand for 2 weeks before using.

FOOD PACKAGING TERMS

Diet ..... Contains no more than 40 calories per serving. Also may have at least a third fewer calories than the product it replaces or resembles.

Extra lean ...... Denotes meat and poultry products that have no more than 5% fat by weight.

Lean ...... On meat and poultry products, indicates no more than 10% fat by weight. The term "lean" may be used as part of a brand name with no restriction other than it must have a nutrition label.

Leaner ...... Can be used on meat and poultry products that have 25% less fat than the standard product. It does not necessarily mean, however, that the product is low in fat.

Low calorie ...... Denotes products with no more than 40 calories per serving or 0.4 calories per gram of food.

Reduced calorie ...... Must contain at least a third fewer calories than the product it replaces or resembles. Label must show a comparison between the reduced-calorie product and the standard product.

Sugar free ...... Does not contain sucrose (table sugar) but may contain other sweeteners such as honey, molasses or fructose, all of which add to the total calories and carbohydrates.

Naturally sweetened ...... Food sweetened with a fruit or juice rather than sugar. There is no regulation on this term, though, so a naturally sweetened product can contain sugar or other refined sweetener such as high-fructose corn sweetener.

No salt added, unsalted, without added salt ...... These terms mean no salt was added during processing, but the product may still have high sodium levels due to the use of other sodium-containing ingredients such as sodium phosphate, baking powder or monosodium glutamate.

Sodium free ...... Contains fewer than 5 milligrams of sodium per serving.

Reduced sodium ..... Reduced by at least 75% from usual level of sodium per serving.

Low sodium ...... No more than 140 milligrams of sodium per serving.

Very low sodium ...... Contains 35 or fewer milligrams per serving.

Natural ...... When referring to meat and poultry, means the product contains no artificial flavors, colors, preservatives or synthetic ingredients. No legal definition exists for the "natural" in processed foods; a natural potato chip, for example, can have artificial colors or flavors added.

Naturally flavored ...... Flavoring must be from an extract, oil or other derivative of a spice, herb, root, leaf or other natural source. Naturally flavored products can have artificial ingredients, however.

Organic ...... No legal definition exists. Use of the term is prohibited on meat and poultry products.

No cholesterol ...... May not contain cholesterol but may contain large amounts of saturated fat such as coconut or palm oil, which tend to raise the level of cholesterol in the blood.

Saturated fats ...... Usually harden at room temperature and are found in animal products and some vegetable products. They tend to raise the level of cholesterol in the blood. Saturated animal fats are found primarily in beef, veal, lamb, pork, ham, butter, cream, whole milk and regular cheeses. Saturated vegetable fats are found in solid and hydrogenated shortenings, coconut oil, cocoa butter, palm oil and palm kernel oil.

Hydrogenated fats ...... Fats and oils changed from their natural liquid form to become more solid, such as most margarine and shortening. May be partially or almost completely hydrogenated. Nutritionists generally advise us to avoid completely hydrogentated oils since they resemble saturated fats. Margarines containing partially hydrogenated oils may be acceptable if they contain twice as much polyunsaturated as saturated fat.

DIETARY FIBER IN FOODS

		Amount	Weight (grams)	Fiber (grams)
Breads	Graham crackers	2 squares	14.2	0.4
	Pumpernickel bread	3/4 slice	24	1.4
	Rye bread	1 slice	25	1.7
	Whole wheat bread	1 slice	25	1.9
	Whole wheat crackers	6 crackers	19.8	2.1
	Whole wheat roll	3/4 roll	21	1.5
Fruit	Apple	1/2 large	83	2.1
	Apricots	2	72	1.4
	Banana	1/2 medium	54	1.1
	Blackberries	3/4 cup	108	7.3
	Cantaloupe	1 cup	160	1.6
	Cherries	10 large	68	1.0
	Dates, dried	2	18	1.5
	Figs, dried	1 medium	20	2.2
	Grapes, green	10	50	0.6
	Grapefruit	1/2	87	1.1
	Honeydew	1 cup	170	1.8
	Orange	1 small	78	1.9
	Peach	1 medium	100	1.7
	Pear	1/2 medium	82	2.3
	Pineapple	1/2	78	1.2
	Plums	3 small	85	1.7
	Prunes, dried	2	15	1.4
	Raisins	1 1/2 tbsp.	14	0.8
	Strawberries	1 cup	143	3.7
	Tangerine	1 large	101	2.0
	Watermelon	1 cup	160	0.6
Grains	All Bran	1/3 cup	28	8.5
	Bran Chex	1/2 cup	21	3.9
	Corn Bran	1/2 cup	21	4.0
	Corn Flakes	3/4 cup	21	0.4
	Grapenuts Flakes	2/3 cup	21	1.4
	Grapenuts	3 tbsp.	21	1.4
	Oatmeal	3/4 pkg.	21	2.3
	Shredded Wheat	1 biscuit	21	2.2
	Wheaties	3/4 cup	21	2.0

		Amount	Weight (grams)	Fiber (grams)
Rice	Rice, brown, cooked	1/3 cup	65	1.1
	Rice, white, cooked	1/3 cup	68	0.2
Meat, Milk, Eggs	Beef	1 ounce	28	0.0
	Cheese	3/4 ounce	21	0.0
	Chicken/Turkey	1 ounce	28	0.0
	Cold cuts/Frankfurters	1 ounce	28	0.0
	Eggs	3 large	99	0.0
	Fish	2 ounces	56	0.0
	Ice cream	1 ounce	28	0.0
	Milk	1 cup	240	0.0
	Pork	1 ounce	28	0.0
	Yogurt	5 ounces	140	0.0
Vegetables	Beans, green	1/2 cup	64	1.5
	Beans, string	1/2 cup	55	2.1
	Beets	1/2 cup	85	1.7
	Broccoli	1/2 cup	93	3.1
	Brussels sprouts	1/2 cup	78	3.5
	Cabbage	1/2 cup	85	2.0
	Carrots	1/2 cup	78	2.5
	Cauliflower	1/2 cup	90	2.3
	Celery	1/2 cup	60	1.0
	Cucumber	1/2 cup	70	0.8
	Eggplant	1/2 cup	100	3.4
	Lentils, cooked	1/2 cup	100	5.1
	Lettuce	1 cup	55	0.7
	Mushrooms	1/2 cup	35	0.6
	Onions	1/2 cup	58	0.9
	Potato, baked	1/2 medium	75	1.8
	Radishes	1/2 cup	58	1.3
	Spinach, fresh	1 cup	55	1.8
	Sweet potato, baked	1/2 medium	75	2.3
	Tomato	1 small	100	1.5
	Turnip greens	1/2 cup	93	2.9
	Winter squash	1/2 cup	120	3.4
	Zucchini	1/2 cup	65	0.7

EQUIVALENT CHART

	When the recipe calls for	Use
Baking	1/2 cup butter	4 ounces
	2 cups butter	1 pound
	4 cups all-purpose flour	1 pound
	4 1/2 to 5 cups sifted cake flour	1 pound
	1 square chocolate	1 ounce
	1 cup semisweet chocolate chips	6 ounces
	4 cups marshmallows	1 pound
	2 1/4 cups packed brown sugar	1 pound
	4 cups confectioners' sugar	1 pound
	2 cups granulated sugar	1 pound
Cereal – Bread	1 cup fine dry bread crumbs	4 to 5 slices
	1 cup soft bread crumbs	2 slices
	1 cup small bread cubes	2 slices
	1 cup fine cracker crumbs	28 saltines
	1 cup fine graham cracker crumbs	15 crackers
	1 cup vanilla wafer crumbs	22 wafers
	1 cup crushed cornflakes	3 cups uncrushed
	4 cups cooked macaroni	8 ounces uncooked
	3 1/2 cups cooked rice	1 cup uncooked
Dairy	1 cup shredded cheese	4 ounces
	1 cup cottage cheese	8 ounces
	1 cup sour cream	8 ounces
	1 cup whipped cream	1/2 cup heavy cream
	2/3 cup evaporated milk	1 small can
	1 2/3 cups evaporated milk	1 13-ounce can
Fruit	4 cups sliced or chopped apples	4 medium
	1 cup mashed bananas	3 medium
	2 cups pitted cherries	4 cups unpitted
	3 cups shredded coconut	8 ounces
	4 cups cranberries	1 pound
	1 cup pitted dates	1 8-ounce package
	1 cup candied fruit	1 8-ounce package
	3 to 4 tablespoons lemon juice plus 1 tablespoon grated lemon rind	1 lemon
	1/3 cup orange juice plus 2 teaspoons grated orange rind	1 orange
	4 cups sliced peaches	8 medium
	2 cups pitted prunes	1 12-ounce package
	3 cups raisins	1 15-ounce package

When the recipe calls for	Use
Meats 4 cups chopped cooked chicken 3 cups chopped cooked meat 2 cups cooked ground meat	1 5-pound chicken 1 pound, cooked 1 pound, cooked
Nuts 1 cup chopped nuts	4 ounces shelled 1 pound unshelled
Vegetables 2 cups cooked green beans 2½ cups lima beans or red beans 4 cups shredded cabbage 1 cup grated carrot 8 ounces fresh mushrooms 1 cup chopped onion 4 cups sliced or chopped potatoes 2 cups canned tomatoes	½ pound fresh or 1 16-ounce can 1 cup dried, cooked 1 pound 1 large 1 4-ounce can 1 large 4 medium 1 16-ounce can

Measurement Equivalents

1 tablespoon = 3 teaspoons 2 tablespoons = 1 ounce 4 tablespoons = ¼ cup 5⅓ tablespoons = ⅓ cup 8 tablespoons = ½ cup 12 tablespoons = ¾ cup 16 tablespoons = 1 cup 1 cup = 8 ounces or ½ pint 4 cups = 1 quart 4 quarts = 1 gallon	1 6½ to 8-ounce can = 1 cup 1 10½ to 12-ounce can = 1¼ cups 1 14 to 16-ounce can = 1¾ cups 1 16 to 17-ounce can = 2 cups 1 18 to 20-ounce can = 2½ cups 1 20-ounce can = 3½ cups 1 46 to 51-ounce can = 5¾ cups 1 6½ to 7½-pound can or Number 10 can = 12 to 13 cups

Metric Equivalents

Liquid	Dry
1 teaspoon = 5 milliliters 1 tablespoon = 15 milliliters 1 fluid ounce = 30 milliliters 1 cup = 250 milliliters 1 pint = 500 milliliters	1 quart = 1 liter 1 ounce = 30 grams 1 pound = 450 grams 2.2 pounds = 1 kilogram

NOTE: The metric measures are approximate benchmarks for purposes of home food preparation.

SUBSTITUTION CHART

	Instead of	Use
Baking	1 teaspoon baking powder	1/4 teaspoon soda plus 1/2 teaspoon cream of tartar
	1 tablespoon cornstarch (for thickening)	2 tablespoons flour or 1 tablespoon tapioca
	1 cup sifted all-purpose flour	1 cup plus 2 tablespoons sifted cake flour
	1 cup sifted cake flour	1 cup minus 2 tablespoons sifted all-purpose flour
	1 cup dry bread crumbs	3/4 cup cracker crumbs
Dairy	1 cup buttermilk	1 cup sour milk or 1 cup yogurt
	1 cup heavy cream	3/4 cup skim milk plus 1/3 cup butter
	1 cup light cream	7/8 cup skim milk plus 3 tablespoons butter
	1 cup sour cream	7/8 cup sour milk plus 3 tablespoons butter
	1 cup sour milk	1 cup milk plus 1 tablespoon vinegar or lemon juice or 1 cup buttermilk
Seasoning	1 teaspoon allspice	1/2 teaspoon cinnamon plus 1/8 teaspoon cloves
	1 cup catsup	1 cup tomato sauce plus 1/2 cup sugar plus 2 tablespoons vinegar
	1 clove of garlic	1/8 teaspoon garlic powder or 1/8 teaspoon instant minced garlic or 3/4 teaspoon garlic salt or 5 drops of liquid garlic
	1 teaspoon Italian spice	1/4 teaspoon each oregano, basil, thyme, rosemary plus dash of cayenne
	1 teaspoon lemon juice	1/2 teaspoon vinegar
	1 tablespoon mustard	1 teaspoon dry mustard
	1 medium onion	1 tablespoon dried minced onion or 1 teaspoon onion powder
Sweet	1 1-ounce square chocolate	1/4 cup cocoa plus 1 teaspoon shortening
	1 2/3 ounces semisweet chocolate	1 ounce unsweetened chocolate plus 4 teaspoons granulated sugar
	1 cup honey	1 to 1 1/4 cups sugar plus 1/4 cup liquid or 1 cup corn syrup or molasses
	1 cup granulated sugar	1 cup packed brown sugar or 1 cup corn syrup, molasses or honey minus 1/4 cup liquid

INDEX

ADD TO YOUR COOKBOOK COLLECTION

The *Animaland Cookbook* compiled by Dixie (Mrs. Tom T.) Hall is more than just a cookbook. It is the united effort of people from all walks of life joining hands to benefit All Creatures Great and Small, people and animals.

It is a "purrfectly" "doggone" good collection of favorite recipes which will grace any kitchen and which will make a "tasteful" gift for any occasion. And there are exciting photographs of stars—often with their pets!

All proceeds from the sale of this book will benefit Animaland, a thirty-two acre complex located near Nashville, Tennessee.

The Animaland Cookbook contains recipes from Dolly Parton, Gary Morris, Hank Williams, Jr., George Jones, Waylon Jennings, Minnie Pearl, The Gatlin Brothers, Johnny Cash, President and Rosalyn Carter, Michael Martin Murphey, Jeanne Pruett, Kenny Rogers, Ernest Tubb, Tanya Tucker, The Statler Brothers, Dottie West, Barbara Mandrell and many, many more.

ORDER FORM   *Animaland Cookbook*

To order your copy of the *Animaland Cookbook* please send **$11.95** per book to:

Animaland
P.O. Box 1591
Franklin, TN 37065
Tel. (615) 794-8679

Name _____

Address _____

City _____

State _____

Zip _____

Please send me _____ copy(s) of the *Animaland Cookbook*.

ADD TO YOUR COOKBOOK COLLECTION

Not just another cookbook for people on special diets, but delicious eating for anyone who wants to stay healthy. These delicious low-fat recipes make healthy eating fun and easy for everyone. They were developed by **Lizzie Burt**, Hawaii Ironman Triathlete, Boston marathoner and professional cooking school instructor, and **Nelda Mercer**, Registered Dietitian and the Assistant Director of Preventive Nutrition at the University of Michigan MedSport Cardiac Programs.

High Fit–Low Fat is a 160-page book that includes simple-to-understand information on nutrition, nutritional analysis of each recipe, including diabetic exchanges, and color photographs. Also included are sections for entertaining and special occasions, kid's menu, and a special training table section just for the athlete. All recipes and menu suggestions comply with the American Heart Association's guidelines and the recently published Surgeon General's Report on nutrition.

Eating healthy never tasted so good!